T0328463

Cambridge Elements

Elements in Ancient Philosophy
edited by
James Warren
University of Cambridge

ARISTOTLE ON WOMEN

Physiology, Psychology, and Politics

Sophia M. Connell
Birkbeck College, University of London

CAMBRIDGE
UNIVERSITY PRESS

CAMBRIDGE
UNIVERSITY PRESS

University Printing House, Cambridge CB2 8BS, United Kingdom

One Liberty Plaza, 20th Floor, New York, NY 10006, USA

477 Williamstown Road, Port Melbourne, VIC 3207, Australia

314–321, 3rd Floor, Plot 3, Splendor Forum, Jasola District Centre,
New Delhi – 110025, India

103 Penang Road, #05–06/07, Visioncrest Commercial, Singapore 238467

Cambridge University Press is part of the University of Cambridge.

It furthers the University's mission by disseminating knowledge in the pursuit of
education, learning, and research at the highest international levels of excellence.

www.cambridge.org
Information on this title: www.cambridge.org/9781108713467
DOI: 10.1017/9781108581950

First published 2021

A catalogue record for this publication is available from the British Library.

ISBN 978-1-108-71346-7 Paperback
ISSN 2631-4118 (online)
ISSN 2631-410X (print)

Aristotle on Women

Physiology, Psychology, and Politics

Elements in Ancient Philosophy

DOI: 10.1017/9781108581950
First published online: July 2021

Sophia M. Connell
Birkbeck College, University of London

Author for correspondence: Sophia M. Connell, sophia.connell@bbk.ac.uk

Abstract: This Element provides an account of Aristotle on women that combines what is found in his scientific biology with his practical philosophy. Scholars have often debated how these two fields are related. The current study shows that according to Aristotelian biology, women are set up for intelligence and tend to be milder-tempered than men. Thus, women are not curtailed either intellectually or morally by their biology. The biological basis for the rule of men over women is women's lack of spiritedness. Aristotle's *Politics* must be read with its audience in mind; there is a need to convince men of the importance of avoiding insurrection both in the city and the household. While their spiritedness gives men the upper hand, they are encouraged to listen to the views of free women in order to achieve the best life for all.

Keywords: Aristotle, women, spirit, mothers, virtue

ISBNs: 9781108713467 (PB), 9781108581950 (OC)
ISSNs: 2631-4118 (online), 2631-410X (print)

Contents

1 Introduction and Methodology

Based on evidence from across the Aristotelian Corpus, this Element aims to counter the view that Aristotle, in stark contrast with Plato in his *Republic*, thought women morally and intellectually inferior to men. While, unlike Plato, Aristotle thought of women and men as significantly different, there is more agreement with Plato about the ability of women to achieve the best life than has usually been recognised. Aristotelian principles even suggest that women are well-suited to philosophical pursuits.

The usual starting point for discovering what Aristotle thought about women is *Politics* 1, where he declares that men are natural rulers. The only hint of an explanation for the subordination of women is that their capacity to deliberate is 'unauthoritative' (*akuros*, 1260a13), a 'Delphic'[1] statement that lends itself to numerous interpretations. There are two key schools of thought: an intrapersonal interpretation and an interpersonal interpretation.[2] According to the intrapersonal view, women are physiologically and psychologically impaired by being chronically weak-willed. Their deliberative faculty is not in control internally. According to the interpersonal reading, women are unable to control those outside themselves to make their decisions have any immediate external impact. Interpreters sometimes reach for clues in Aristotle's biological and zoological works for the rationale behind the subordination of women, something beyond a mere statement of fact about their psychological or social condition. If the body is the actualisation of psychological capacities then a different body would appear to point to a different underlying psychology. This Element will provide an analysis of these connections, beginning with the bodies of women in Aristotle's biological works as reproductive and sentient, before turning to female psychology and character. It will then turn to Aristotelian practical philosophy. My central conclusion is that Aristotle's claims about women in this section of the *Politics* have been misunderstood and that this misunderstanding has excessively influenced the general picture of Aristotle's attitude to women.

Aristotle did not write a treatise on women.[3] His remarks on female human beings range broadly across works on zoology, embryology, anatomy, politics, rhetoric, ethics, and literary theory. We find information about the make-up of male and female bodies in Aristotle's embryology, where he describes their conception and formation, the male ending up drier, larger, and more sinewy.[4] Another place to look for more information about the bodily condition of women is Aristotle's account of the sense organs (*Sens.* 1.436b18–437a16, *Juv.* 3.461a10–21; *DA*

---

[1] Pangle (2013: 68).   [2] Terminology first employed by Fortenbaugh (1977).
[3] Levy (1990: 397); Mulgan (1994).   [4] Connell (2016: ch. 8.3).

2.19.421a17–22, *PA* 2.16.660a11–13). The next area of his biological thought of interest is the account of the consistency of blood, where Aristotle is explicit about the differences between male and female varieties (*PA* 2.2). And finally, the *History of Animals* gives an account of the character and intellectual capacities of female as opposed to male animals and contains a small section on women's character (*HA* 8.1).[5]

Before a detailed analysis of Aristotle's texts, it is helpful to give the explanatory framework in which these discussions occur. The *HA* provides broad facts about males and females that Aristotle has either observed in their natural setting or heard from other thinkers.[6] What we get here resonates with ideas found in Greek literature at the time about the character of women and the frustrations their subordinated lives often entail. Thus, women are said to be sensitive, compassionate, caring, and intelligent as well as scheming and spiteful. Aristotle's other works on biology and physiology are explanatory rather than merely descriptive, but none focus on explaining sex differences. There is also no explanatory account of ethology, that is, animal character, in the section of *HA* where the statements about women's characters occur. Thus, any attempt to provide Aristotle's reasons for these variations remains speculative.

The *Generation of Animals* provides two explanations of sex difference, one in terms of final causes and another in terms of material causes, the backdrop being that although the separation of male and female animals is 'for the better' in one way, it is also accidental in another way.[7] Many of the physical variations between the sexes are not for any purpose in nature but are side effects of generative functions.

The *Parts of Animals* is focused on the functionality of body parts. Overall, the account is about what is 'for the best' and thus one can find that blood consistency facilitates intelligence and character for all human beings according to their rational essence (*EN* 1.7). The accidental differences in blood consistency between members of the same kind, which are non-teleological, can be used to help account for the differences between the capacities and potential characters of men and women noted in the *HA*; these differences will be very slight.

While Aristotle's biological works seek theoretical knowledge, his practical philosophy is prescriptive, aiming to improve the lives of people in communities. Aristotle's ethical works are written for a male audience and prescribe the best life in terms of active virtues and theoretical activities. The *Politics* is

---

[5] I follow the numbering of the Books of the *Historia Animalium* restored by Balme (Aristotle 1991a).

[6] These are preliminary *historiai* of the differentiae of animals (Karbowski 2014b: 100).

[7] Connell (2016: ch. 8).

concerned with a citizen population's best life: virtue and happiness (*Pol.* 7.1.1323a23–34; 1323b20–35). Citizens are often the minority in a given community and consist of those capable of sharing in rule and political judgement (*Pol.* 3.1.1275b17–20; 3.6.1279a9–13). The idea of citizenship is fluid and can include women as well as men.[8] The work assumes that the role of women in the aims of a good government is to be citizen wives, participating in heterosexual partnerships with a view to procreation and the raising of citizen children. Aristotle's style in these works is looser than in the scientific ones. He quotes from literature, for example poetry, in an attempt to engage the men training for and currently involved in legislative and political life.

It is important to realise that Aristotle does not have a reductive view of human emotional and cognitive capacities. Humans are deliberative (*HA* 1.1.488b24), which means that they are in principle able to control even extreme desires (*EN* 7.5.1149a12–16). They determine their lives through reason and are not at the mercy of their bodies like other animals are.[9]

2 Aristotle's Account of the Female Body

This section begins with a description of how sexual differentiation at conception results in differently textured bodies. It will then discuss the subsequent differences in the heart, sense organs, blood, and overall bodily structure. To what degree these differences are functional rather than accidental will be touched on before ending with some general comments on the condition of female bodies in Aristotle's biology.

It is Aristotle's usual procedure to note and analyse differences between types, starting at the broadest grouping and ending with 'ultimate species' (*atoma eidē*, *PA* 1.1). Males and females within a kind have the same form and so sex difference exists below the level of species (*GA* 1.23.730b33–34b1; *Metaph.* 10.9). The philosophical reason for documenting these differences is to elucidate reproduction. In aid of this, the *HA* collects data on morphological differences, times of sexual maturity (5.14), mating habits (5.2–8), gestational lengths, and numbers of young per birth (*HA* 5.15–20, 33; 6). Other differences

---

[8] Citizens in some cities are the children of male and female citizens (*Pol.* 3.2.1275b22–3). This is said to be Pericles' law at *Ath. Pol.* 26.4. Both children and women can be free, which is why 'political activity is neither a necessary nor a sufficient condition of being a free person for Aristotle' (Lockwood 2018: 109). Aristotle also mentions the possibility that citizens be those that carry arms (*Pol.* 4.13.1297a41–b1) or hold office (3.1.1275a19–23), but commentators do not think that he believes these requirements are absolutely necessary for citizenship. See Kraut (1997: 133).

[9] '[H]uman beings do many things against habit and nature, if reason persuades them that they ought' (*Pol.* 7.12.1332b6–8). Deslauriers (2009) argues that the idea of the body determining the powers of rational soul is an untenable interpretation of Aristotle (220–23).

between males and females within a kind include size, strength, presence of defensive organs, temperament, character, skill, ability to learn, and capacity for intelligent action (*HA* 4–8). These differences are not so clearly related to reproduction and look to be side effects of teleologically directed processes.

2.1 The Reproductive Body of a Woman

Male and female animals differ from the point of conception, which is a colder mixture in the case of the female (*GA* 4.1–2). This affects the formation of the first part in the embryo, the heart, where the nutritive soul resides and which brings about the construction of the rest of the bodily parts (*GA* 2.4.740a15–21). Although male and female animals very often have morphological and physiological differences when fully developed, the fundamental difference between them is in their hearts (*GA* 4.1.766a35–b5).[10] Due to their hearts' different heating capacities, they are ultimately distinguished by their ability to concoct the final nourishment into male semen (e.g. *GA* 1.20.728a18–25; 4.1.766a30–33). Female animals are unable to do this, instead producing a less concocted, colder generative residue that serves as material (*GA* 2.4.738a37–b3). Foetal development in both the male and female proceeds from a network of blood vessels that form a framework for the rest of the body (*GA* 2.6.743a1–3; *PA* 3.5.668b24–6). Aristotle thinks that blood contains all the parts of the body potentially, being the ultimate nourishment (*GA* 1.19.726b1, 2.4.740a21; *PA* 2.2.651a15, 4.4.678a7). This blood can then be carried to each extremity and the bodily parts formed from it. Male animals will have hearts that are better able to concoct and so the blood will be more compacted and thicker, which will make their blood vessels tougher and their flesh harder (*HA* 4.11.538a22–b24).[11]

This accords with certain data in Aristotle's zoology; that is, that female animals tend on the whole to be smaller[12] and to have less energy (*HA* 8.1.608b12–15). In supporting his idea that menstrual blood is the female animal's spermatic contribution, Aristotle proposes that the more delicate appearance of female bodies is due to residues being bled out of the body rather than being used to construct and maintain a stronger, more sinewy one.

---

[10] Connell (2016: 270–80); Deslauriers (2009: 217–18).

[11] Leunissen takes this to mean that female bodies are for Aristotle 'less shaped in accordance with the species form as realised in the male' (2017: 149), but there isn't any evidence for female animals being incomplete in the sense of their body parts remaining unshaped. As Aristotle puts it, an animal is complete once it has a male or female body (*GA* 2.4.737b10–12; see also *GA* 1.1.715a20–21). While he does talk about the female as incomplete, this is with respect to the ability to concoct semen into its final form, i.e. male semen, and not with respect to the articulation of her own body parts (Connell 2016: 118–19).

[12] Exceptions include fish, insects, and egg-laying quadrupeds (*HA* 4.11.538b24–8; *GA* 1.16.721a17–20).

Furthermore, females are not veiny in the same way as males are and they are finer (*glaphurōtera*)[13] and smoother (*leiotera*) because the residue going towards those [characteristics/parts] is discharged together in the menses. (*GA* 1.19.727a15–18)[14]

Due both to initial development and subsequent physiology, female animals generally have more delicate flesh.[15] The same ideas explain why females have less bodily bulk (1.19.727a19), smoother bodies, and tend to lack external parts such as hair, horns, and tusks (*HA* 4.11.538b15–24; *PA* 3.1.661b31–662a5). Furthermore, it seems that female flesh is 'smoother' because there is more fluid in it (*hugrosarkotera*; *HA* 4.11.538b9). This follows from the fact that the female heart will not dry up the flesh as much as the male heart does.

In *On the Parts of Animals* Aristotle states that blood consistency affects character and sensation (2.4.651a13–14). Due to a heart that is less able to concoct, female blood will be more plentiful and thinner, leading to tendencies towards fearfulness.

> Those with very watery fluid are more fearful. For fear is a cooling. Having such a blend in the heart, the way is prepared for this feeling. (*PA* 2.4.650b27–30)

Boldness is associated with thick blood. Just as fear chills, temper heats. Earthier blood retains and builds this heat, becoming 'like embers in the blood' (651a3). These fibres, when combined with heat, thicken the blood, making animals more prone to boldness and quick locomotive reactions (*PA* 2.2.648a2). Female blood lacks these earthy fibres. This relative lack of fibres means that female blood is less able to support boldness. But this also means that it is more fluid and 'purer', facilitating perceptive sensitivity and intelligence.[16]

> It happens that some of these animals [with thin blood] have very fine (*glathurōteran*) intelligence (*dianoia*), not because of the coldness of blood but due to its being thinner and pure. For those [animals] with thinner and purer fluid have a more mobile perception (*eukinētoteran* … *aisthēsin*). (*PA* 2.4.650b18–24)

---

[13] Aristotle uses this term to mean something elegant, precise, refined, or smooth; see, for example, *HA* 5.27.555b11; *PA* 3.1.662b8. Cf. *Phgn.* 5.809b5–7.

[14] All translations are mine unless otherwise indicated.

[15] Their flesh will differ because their blood vessels do (*GA* 4.1.764b28–33).

[16] Leunissen's idea that female blood makes female animals less intelligent than male animals comes from one passage at *HA* 3.19.521a23, which states that female blood is 'thicker and blacker' than male blood (2017: xxviii, 154). I take it this refers to external menses. One difficulty for her interpretation is that the female blood cannot be both 'thick' and unconcocted, since concoction is what causes the thickening.

Sex differences for Aristotle, then, include the heating capacity of the heart, the texture of flesh, body size, external parts, and the consistency of blood (or its analogue). Male and female animals also develop different reproductive and copulatory organs (*GA* 1.2–11.716a24–721a26), which are for the ends of generation. Sexed variations in other body parts are comparable to differences that one might find within a kind more generally. For example, blue jays' wings might vary slightly in length or colour due to the material conditions in which they were initially constructed. In the case of blood consistency, these are parts that form and continue to be produced after birth, like hair and nails (*GA* 2.6.745a11–16). Because it is constantly being remade, blood is affected by environmental factors such as diet and climate. Although blood consistency is required for the type of animal in each instance,[17] minor variations (whether maintained throughout life or changing within a lifetime) are accidental.

2.2 The Sentient Body of a Woman

In general, Aristotle thinks that humans (both men and women) have the right sort of heat in their heart to facilitate intelligence (*GA* 2.6.744a30–31). Cognitive capacities are not only affected by the blood and heart but also by the nature of the sense organs.[18] These organs are the channels by which animals represent and experience the external world. Sensing is a sort of knowing (*GA* 1.23.731a33–4); the more and better an animal's senses, the better it is able to know.

There are two ways in which the senses can be measured for effectiveness – their distance capacity and their ability to discern differences or detail (*GA* 5.1.780b12–17). Humans are best at 'accurately perceiving the differences in the objects perceived' (*GA* 5.2.781b19; see also *HA* 1.15.494b16–17). This is due to the fact that 'in humans the sense organ is pure and the least earthy and corporeal, and besides that, nature has given them, for their size, the thinnest skin of any animal' (781b19–22; Cf. *GA* 5.5.785b8–9). The thinness of the skin in humans ensures that each of their sense organs is more sensitive (*DA* 2.9.421a17–26; *PA* 2.16.660a11–13; 2.13.657a33–4). Skin covers the eye (*GA* 5.1.780b22–9), ear (5.2.781b17–23), the inside of the nose (5.7.781b1–6), and the sensitive flesh on their bodies by which they perceive the sense objects of touch. Good vision depends on the skin (on the pupil) being thin (*GA* 5.1.780a26–9). Furthermore, Aristotle is clear that 'to hear and smell accurately means to perceive as well as possible all the differences in the objects

---

17 For blood consistency as teleological see Deslauriers (2009) and Connell (2018).

18 Knowledge is crucially linked to perception (*Metaph.* 1.1.980a22–30). Furthermore, the rational faculty depends on the faculty of imagination based on perception (*DA* 3.8.432a4–9; *Mem.* 1.449b31–450a1).

perceived'. With these senses also, 'the ability to perceive the differences well' is due to the sense organ, 'just as it is in the case of sight, being pure and clean itself, and so must the membrane round it' (*GA* 5.2.781a17–21).

The ability to discern differences more accurately is directly related to intelligence and said to be the result not only of thin skin but also of soft flesh:

> With respect to touch, humans discriminate more accurately than other animals. For this reason, the human is the most intelligent (*phronimōtatos*) of the animals. A sign of this is that within humankind, people are clever or dim according to the sense organ [of touch] and according to no other. For those with hard flesh are naturally dim and those with soft flesh (*malakosarkoi*) are naturally intelligent. (*DA* 2.9.421a20–26)

Female animals generally, and women in particular, have thinner skin and softer flesh than their male counterparts.[19] Leunissen states that female sense organs are 'hard' and insensitive. However, Aristotle clearly considers the largest and most important sense organ, the skin, to be smoother and softer in females.[20] This means that female human beings, according to Aristotelian biology, are better arranged for the perceptual accuracy necessary for intelligence than men are.[21] Another possible effect of this extra sensitivity is that female animals generally, including female human beings, feel pleasure and pain more, or more acutely. Aristotle never explicitly says this, but when it comes to moral weaknesses, it is implied that women are more prone to err due to their bodily desire for pleasure and the absence of pain.[22] This might also mean that they feel more, or more acutely, other bodily pleasures such as those gained from painting, music, and the smell of flowers (*EN* 3.10.1118a2–11).

Another aspect of the condition of women is their bodily proportions. Part of what makes it possible for human beings to be intelligent is the structure of their body and its subsequent orientation.

> Human beings are the only animals that stand upright, and this is because their nature and essence is divine. Now the business of that which is more divine is to think and to be intelligent; and this would not be easy if there were a great deal of the body at the top weighing it down, for weight hampers the

---

[19] Generalising across animal kinds, the author of the *Physiognomics* notes that 'when flesh is hard and constitutionally firm, it indicates dullness of sense' (806b21). This text also provides a feminine picture of the 'good natural parts' including 'rather moist and tender flesh' and 'a thin skin' (807b11–16).

[20] Leunissen (2017: 155–6) actually needs this point to support her claim that woman are congenitally akratic (due to 'softness', see Section 4 below).

[21] Leunissen says that, for Aristotle, women's sense organs are 'developed less well and are therefore functionally inferior', but her reference is to *HA* 4.11.538b2–7, which is about defensive organs, such as horns and tusks, and not sense organs (Leunissen 2017: 154).

[22] See Section 4.

motion of the intellect and of the common sense. (*PA* 4.10.686a27–32, after Peck trans.)

While all humans have this upright posture, because female humans are lighter on top, they are even better shaped for intellectual pursuits. As Aristotle explains, those who are more 'dwarf-like in nature' are 'deficient with respect to possessing intellect' (*PA* 4.10.686b23–7). This condition is when upper portions of the body are large (686b3–23), which is generally true of males.

> In all animals the upper and front parts of the males are better, stronger and more fully equipped than the females, in some females the rear and lower parts are stronger. This also applies to human beings. (*HA* 4.11.538b2–5)[23]

The upper portions of the male body are more developed; 'the male is more dwarf-like than the female' (*Long.* 6.747a32–3). Ergo, males are deficient with respect to possessing intellect in comparison with females.[24]

The human body must be a particular way, structurally and physiologically, in order to facilitate intelligence. This capacity is what distinguishes humans from other animals and, although there is no particular organ of the body in which it is actualised, a human body, with its sensitive flesh and senses, upright orientation, and organs that allow for speech and rational communication, are required.[25] Women have all the structures and organs needed, and in some ways their bodies are better arranged than those of males.

2.3 Women's Bodies as Teleological: A Critique

A well-regarded contemporary theory proposes that differences between men, women, and natural slaves are designed by nature to allow for political communities. The idea is that nature, which aims to bring about the *polis*, divides human beings into 'functional distinct subgroups'.[26] This section will explain why this is not a viable way to connect Aristotle's biology to his politics. The first reason to be cautious about natural purposes for sub-kinds within a species is that Aristotle does not normally explain accidental variations within a kind in terms of his essentialist teleology. Admittedly, sex difference does aim towards the broader ends of generation in all kinds in which it exists. The main features

---

[23] All translations of *HA* 4–6 are from Peck (1970).

[24] Aristotle says that those with dwarf-like proportions have poor memories (*Mem.* 2.453a32–b3). See also *Phgn.*, where it is noted that 'a good memory is signified when the upper parts are disproportionately small and are delicate' (5.808b9–10). Leunissen (2017: 153) thinks that women are more dwarf-like than men, but the texts contradict that conclusion. I thank Mor Segev for this insight.

[25] Connell (2021). The only difference in terms of speech is a higher pitch of voice (*HA* 4.11.538b13–14; *GA* 5.7.786b17–18).

[26] Karbowski (2012, 2014b, 2019).

required for this are the generative parts and the capacities to produce the differentiated generative products (seeds).[27] The differences between male and female bodies extend beyond these and include, as noted above, the textures, temperature, and structures of those bodies. In human beings, Aristotle occasionally notes that different climates and localities produce groups or types of people that differ from one another (*Pol.* 7.7). Is it the case that differences such as these, between the sexes and between people living in different localities,[28] are intended by nature in order that humans reach their ends?

The view that these differences are teleological rests on the idea that *polis*-dwelling is a constraint on our species that means that it can't make all humans rational to the same degree. Thus, 'nature will have to engender human beings with different natural talents, skills, and ultimately rational aptitudes in order to have enough people suited to the various tasks of the polis'.[29] These groups are then likened to the sorts of bees produced through a series of generations: king, worker, and drone.[30]

> So that it happens that the leaders, i.e. kings, generate the same [as themselves], and generate another kind (this is the 'bee' kind [i.e. workers]), and bees generate another [kind], drones, but do not generate their own kind, but they are deprived of this. Since that which is according to nature always has an order, because of this, drones are necessarily deprived of generating even another kind.[31] This very thing appears to happen. For they are generated but generate no other, but generation will have its limit in the third number. And thus this is finely/beautifully established by nature so that these kinds always remain in existence and never fail, though not all generate. (*GA* 3.10.760a27–b2)

The comparison with bee generation works as follows: just as there are three types of bee to do different jobs in the hive and this is part of their 'nature', so also – it is claimed – there are three different types of human being for Aristotle.

> [N]ature must distribute different tasks in the polis and the household to different individuals. This implies that mankind (*anthrōpos*) will naturally divide into subkinds with different roles in the household and the polis, just as

---

[27] On females as teleological see Connell (2016: ch. 8.5–6).

[28] Aristotle also notes variations within kinds in other animals due to differences in locality or climate (*HA* 7.8; 7.13.598b31–599a1; 7.19, 28–9).

[29] Karbowski (2012: 341–2). Compare Aldous Huxley, *Brave New World* (1932): 'We decant our babies as socialized human beings, as Alphas or Epsilons, as future sewage workers or future … He was going to say "future World controllers," but correcting himself, said "future Directors of Hatcheries," instead'. For Karbowski, Aristotelian nature is like the designer of the hatcheries.

[30] Karbowski (2019: 222). Aristotle called the queen bee the 'king'.

[31] Aristotle thinks that animals can generate another unlike the parent only up to three generations, otherwise this would go on to infinity, which is impossible (*GA* 1.1.715b12–16).

bees fall into natural subcategories with distinct roles in the hive. (Karbowski 2019: 227)[32]

However, the comparison of human men, women, and slaves with three types of bee is questionable. For Aristotle, bees' method of generation keeps its three types in existence: kings produce kings and drones; drones produce workers, and workers are infertile. Bees' way of reproducing is fine or beautiful because it accords with mathematical proportion (*GA* 3.10.760a12–13). This 'caste-system' is unique in nature, which is what makes bees 'divine'.[33] A pattern of triple breeding is simply not the case for humans or any other animal. In the generation of animals, there are certain aspects of human reproduction that are singled out, notably their uniquely variable gestational period (*HA* 9.4.584a36–b1; *GA* 4.4.772b7–8; 776a22), but the morphology of two sexes that is produced in each generation is not at all unusual.

There are many other social animals; some are even political (e.g. cranes, *HA* 1.1.488a8; 9.10.614b18–30). In all of these, there is differentiation between male and female. But this does not entail different tasks for each. This makes the fact of the *polis* a much stronger 'natural' consideration in morphological and psychological development in humans than is evident in the texts.[34] Furthermore, to fit to a rigid teleological programme, the 'female' type of human on this reading should ideally be unable to undertake anything but simple means–ends reasoning, so as to be completely under the control of her husband. But, in fact, she has a deliberative capacity. And 'why did nature, which is supposed to do nothing in vain . . . give her a deliberative faculty at all' if she wasn't supposed to use it?[35]

The next problem is that there are both male and female slaves. If nature were really intent on producing three types of human, designed to carry out particular tasks, then men should produce men and women and women should produce slaves, who are themselves unable to breed; this would be just like the case of bees. Instead, women produce both men and women and slaves can reproduce since they also produce both men and women; and in any case, the 'generation' of slaves does not seem possible since those with the bodily morphology of slave are 'often' not slaves and vice versa (*Pol.* 1.5.1254b25–38). There is

---

[32] I mostly engage with Karbowski (2019) as it is the most up-to-date version of this position. Very similar points are made in Karbowski (2012, 2014a).

[33] Lehoux (2019).

[34] There is no space here to argue against the idea of the *polis* as essential to humans; however, we may note that 'For a human is more by nature a coupling (*sunduastikon*) than a political (*politikon*) being' (*EN* 8.12.1162a17–18), and Aristotle only evokes the management of the household: 'it is absurd to argue, from the analogy of animals, that men and women should follow the same pursuits, for animals have not to manage a household' (*Pol.* 2.5.1264b4–6).

[35] Scott (2010: 115).

a strong case for slavery, on Aristotle's view, lasting only one generation.[36] Thus the 'slave' type is not a consistent natural variation. Another problem with the bee comparison is that slave men and women can reproduce with free men and women. The different kinds of bee cannot breed with each other.[37]

If nature were really intent on dividing humans into three types, why wouldn't it do so directly and obviously, as in bees, rather than hijacking sex difference? Indeed, if humans were divided in that way, Aristotelian political organisation would look much more like Plato's communism, with workers, auxiliaries, and leaders living in three different classes (*Rep.* 4). In that scenario, which lines up much better with a beehive, men and women do the same tasks because sex difference is not the difference that is relevant for the assignment of different tasks (*Rep.* 5).

The only place where Aristotle actually talks about natural differences that relate to political tasks is with reference to younger and older people.

> The legislator should investigate the question of how this is to be achieved, and how they should share with one another. We discussed this earlier, for nature itself settled the choice by making part of the same species younger and part older, the former fit to be ruled and the latter to rule. (7.14.1332b34–7; trans. Lockwood 2018)[38]

If Aristotle had thought that, similarly, nature determines the tasks of men and women in the *polis*, it is curious that he never mentions this. Although it is natural in some sense for men to rule over women, this is far more complicated than a division made by nature to determine their character traits and functions. Bees may be designed that way, but in human beings, nurture, education, and rationality must all come about so that women realise their virtues in a political setting.

The final problem for this interpretation is that it requires female human beings to be less intellectually able than males,[39] but the evidence from Aristotle's biological works take us in the opposite direction. Both practically and theoretically, the operations of reason ultimately depend on perceptions and the workings of lower cognition, which depend on the state of the body.[40] The

---

[36] Pellegrin (2013: 100–101; 106–7; 113) explains how, for Aristotle, the descendants of slaves will be integrated into the non-slave population because 'time has ethical effects'.

[37] The 'strong evidence' from the biological works 'that they informed Aristotle's . . . hierarchical anthropological theory' is exaggerated (Karbowski 2019: 222).

[38] The earlier passage reads: 'Nature has given the distinction [of superior and inferior] by making the group that is itself the same in race partly younger and partly older, of which two sets it is appropriate to the one to be governed and for the other to govern' (*Pol.* 7.13.1332b35–8).

[39] Karbowski (2014b: 103): 'women are naturally less intelligent than men'.

[40] Connell (2021).

sensitivity of women's sense organs, the softness of their skin, and the thinness of their blood indicate an even more acute awareness of the sorts of differences required for theoretical and practical reasoning. Nature did not intend this; these variations appear to be accidental – softness of flesh and thinness of skin on sense organs are not clearly necessary for the goal of reproduction. Instead, they are side effects of the need for the female to produce menstrual discharges. In other animals, this also means that females are less likely to have defensive organs and will have smaller upper parts – again features that mean that they will be more acutely aware of their surroundings and have a more sensitive nature. In terms of their bodies, then, female human beings are just as set up for intelligence as males, if not more so.[41]

3 The Character of a Woman

3.1 Character Tendencies in Female Animals

In *HA* 8, before detailing fierce and aggressive tendencies and behaviours (the rest of *HA* 8.1.608b19–35), gentle and friendly ones (8.2), slowness (8.3), intelligence, and other character traits, Aristotle makes his infamous remarks about the differences between male and female character (*HA* 8.1.608a21–b18). 'In all which come to be male and female, nature has established almost the same character of females as opposed to males'.[42] Females are softer (*malakōteron*), quicker to tame, more receptive of handling, and find it easier to learn (*mathēmatikōteron*). Strikingly, the term here derives from *manthanein*, which is primarily used of higher learning (e.g. *Ph.* 2.2.193b31; *EN* 4.8.1142a17; *Metaph.* 6.1.1026a14).[43] 'For example', he writes, 'female Laconian hounds are in fact cleverer (*euphuesterai*) than males'. So far, it does not seem that the natural affective tendencies of female animals are negative; females are more co-operative and quick-witted.

The next section reads:

> All females are less spirited (*athumotera*) than males, except the bear and the leopard. In these the female is thought to be braver. In the other kinds, the females are softer (*malakōtera*), more vicious (*kakourgotera*), less simple (*hētton hapla*), more impetuous (*propetestera*), more thoughtfully concerned about the nurture of the young (*peri tōn teknōn trophēn phronistikōtera*);

---

[41] See also Swanson (1992: 61 and 63): '[*nous*] is facilitated more by a female than by a male nature'. Modrak (1994: 209): 'Insofar as human rationality is dependent on the body, more specifically on the perceptual system, there would appear to be no obvious difference between the sexes'.

[42] All translations of *HA* 7–10 are from Balme's translation of Aristotle (1991a) (sometimes modified).

[43] Nielsen (2015: 579) remarks that this is 'a striking reversal of prejudice'.

males, contrariwise (*enantiōs*), are more spirited (*thumōdestera*), wilder (*agriōtera*), simpler, less cunning (*hētton epiboula*) (608a33–b4).[44]

These differences in behaviour between the sexes are not universal; in some animals, females will be bolder and braver (e.g. in the bear and leopard). There are some female animals that are more energetic, such as the female spider, which does all of the hunting (*HA* 8.39.623a24). Meanwhile, some male animals care for the young as attentively as do the females (e.g. swallows and pigeons, 8.7.612b18–613a1); indeed, human beings also fit into that class (*GA* 3.2.753a7–10). In certain varieties of animal, males alone love and raise the young (e.g. Aristotle's catfish, *HA* 8.37.621a20–b2).

Within a kind, the extent of variation between the sexes in these tendencies is likely to be very slight compared with differences between kinds. Aristotle initially sets out characters (*ēthē*) in *HA* 1.1.488b3–28, where he gives examples of various types of animals and their typical character dispositions. The cow is 'gentle, sluggish, non-aggressive' (*praa, dusthuma, ouk enstatika*); the wild boar is ferocious (*agrios*), aggressive, and stubborn (*amathēs*); the deer and hare are intelligent and timid; the fox is fierce (*agria*) and scheming (*epiboula*). The differences within a kind between the sexes will be slight. For example, the male hare will be slightly less intelligent and slightly less timid than its female counterpart and the female boar will be slightly less ferocious, but each will still have these characteristics predominantly. They will not differ enough to cross to the other side of the spectrum and take on the characters of other animals (e.g. the female boar will not be timid). The snake and wolf are both 'scheming' (*epiboula*), so although this is a characteristic assigned to female animals, all this need mean is that male snakes and wolves are slightly less inclined to be scheming than their female counterparts. If the kind is a spirited one, such as the pig or cow, it will be only slightly less spirited than the male of the kind. Human beings as a kind are the most intelligent, spirited, tameable, and friendly, despite slight variations in these propensities between the sexes.

At *HA* 8.1.608a33–b3, Aristotle says that females are 'less spirited' (*athumotera*), males 'more spirited' (*thumōdestera*).[45] Females and males also differ with respect to tameness/wildness that is broader than gentle/fierce, intelligent/slow witted, fearful/bold but is related to these. All these scales of affective tendencies correspond with a general contrast between spirited/stupid versus

---

[44] This description has parallels in the pseudo-Aristotelian *Physiognomics*, although that text is more dogmatic in not mentioning any exceptions. 'In all beasts that we try to breed the female is tamer and gentler in disposition than the male, less powerful, more easily manageable (*tas cheiroētheias*) (1936b). One may conclude from this that the female has a less spirited temper (*athumotera*)' (5.809a30–34, trans. Loveday/Forster).

[45] For a clear account of this see Leunissen 2017: 16–17.

lacking in spirit/intelligent. Male animals will have harder flesh, which is associated with dullness of the senses (*DA* 2.9.421a17–22; *Phgn.* 2.806b6). Courage was often considered by the Greeks to be the least thoughtful of the virtues.[46] Other traits mentioned here map onto the spectrum of intelligence: females are 'less simple' and 'more thoughtfully concerned about the nurture of the young', while males are 'simpler'. The general idea of females as more intelligent in some sense fits with their being 'quicker to tame' (*HA* 8.1.608a25–6). The learning involved in taming will be more straightforward for females (e.g. *HA* 1.1.448a28–9; 8.46.630b18–22). Furthermore, the term *phronēsis*, which is reserved for human beings in the ethical works (*EN* 6.13), is used in the *HA* of the intellectual capacities of many non-human animals.[47] The thoughtfulness of parents, and female ones in particular, is very much apparent.[48]

The intelligence of female animals in this passage is characterised as a pseudo-moral failing.[49] Females are 'softer' (*malakōtera*). *Malakōs* can mean soft to the touch (*HA* 1.1.486b9–10); female animals do have softer flesh, which Aristotle links here to a gentler nature. The term 'more vicious' (*kakourgotera*) cannot be interpreted without overtones of evildoing; it is also used of fraudulence (Plato *Laws* 933e) and unfair argumentation (*Rh.* 3.2.1404b38–9), and this fits with the female being 'less simple' (*hētton hapla*), as in less frank and open. Instead, there is the implication of slyness or cunning (*epiboula*).[50] There is a tendency to associate female intelligence with 'plotting' (*epiboula*). The idea that females are 'more impetuous' (*propetestera*) is, however, surprising, given that they are less spirited, less inclined to action, and more thoughtful.

---

[46] Which explains in part why Plato has to spend so much time trying to convince his audience that courage could be a kind of knowledge (e.g. *Prot.* 349d–360e).

[47] As with 'action' (*praxis*), Aristotle has a broader use for this term in his *Historia Animalium* and a narrower, more technical sense in his ethical works. For 'action' see especially *HA* 487a11–488b10; Aristotle restricts the term to human beings at *EN* 6.2.1139a17–20. One might also say this of other terms used in the *HA*, such as 'friendship' (8.1.609b33; 610a8–13), 'political' (1.1.488a3–11; 7.1.589a2), 'war' (608b19–610a34), which, without the addition of rationality, animals cannot fully participate in.

[48] For example the doe (8.5.611a16), female bear (8.6.612a2), and female partridge (613b32f.). *Phronēsis* in animals is also associated with hunting and self-medicating (e.g. 8.5.611a18, 612a4). Females can excel in other activities requiring skill, such as the spider, which is very wise (*sophōtatos*) when it hunts (8.39.623a8).

[49] Non-human animals cannot be good or bad, so these terms are being used in an extended fashion. As Aristotle explains it, the animal world contains 'traces' (*ichnē*, 7.1.588a19; 8.1.608b4) of human-sounding characteristics. Although it is difficult to deny that the passages attribute somewhat superior cognitive capacities to female animals, most conclude that these are only viewed negatively by Aristotle. See especially Mayhew (2004: 94–5): 'this passage does not paint a positive picture of female cognition'.

[50] The male is less 'cunning': the Greek term *epiboula* comes from *epibouleuō* – to plot against (*EN* 7.6.1149b13), with connotations of treachery (Plato, *Rep.* 566b, *Tht.* 174d). See also *Phgn.* 5, where the male is said to be braver and more 'honest' and the female cowardly and 'less honest' (809b13–14).

As for the male character, this relates not only to the degree of their spirit (*thumos*) but also to the broader spectrum of tame/wild. Aristotle thinks of male and female in some sense as contraries (*enantia*). On this score, they differ by the more and the less, so that male animals will have more *thumos*, that is, be more spirited, honour-loving, and prone to angry outbursts, and also more wild (*agriotera*, *HA* 8.1.608b3), that is, untamed, fierce, savage, and akin to those animals that wage wars (*HA* 8.1.608b19–35).

3.2 Character Tendencies in Women

Sexually differentiated character traits are most evident (*phaneroteras*), Aristotle says, in human beings, not simply because they are more accessible to observation[51] but also because humans are 'more complete' (*HA* 8.1.608b7–8):

> Thus a woman is more compassionate (*eleemonesteron*) and more prone to tears than a man, furthermore, more jealous and complaining and more apt to scold and hit out. The female is also more dispirited (*dusthumon*) and despondent (*duselpi*) than the male, is more shameless and lying, more inclined to deceive and has a longer memory; furthermore, she is more wakeful, more afraid of action and on the whole less inclined to move than the male, and she takes less food. The male, on the other hand, is more ready to help and braver than the female, as even in the soft-bodied kind when the sepia is struck by a trident, the male helps the female, but the female flees when the male is struck. (*HA* 8.1.608b8–18)

A woman, for Aristotle, is colder, smaller, and has thinner blood than a man. This explains the need for less food. The disinclination to move could be seen in a positive light as being more 'stable'.[52] Women's extra-sensitive sense organs fit with a better and longer memory.[53] The cooler, more fluid body will also help to explain some of the affective tendencies listed: a woman will lie more towards the mild or gentle side of the spectrum and so is more compassionate and more likely to cry (maybe also due to the relative fluidity of her blood). The rest of the attributes indicate a lack of spirit and, if anything, an excess of intelligence in a way that suggests moral pathology. Rather than simply being less spirited, as in non-human animals, women are *bad* spirited (*dusthumia*). And their intelligence isn't simply scheming but inclines towards lying and deception. The political implications of this presentation of female character will be explored in Section 5. For the time being, the clear message is that

---

[51] We must study what is more familiar to us first (*Ph.* 1.1.184a16–24). Humans are most familiar (*HA* 1.6.491a20–23).
[52] Dodds (1996: 84).   [53] Memories are phantasmic traces of perceptions (Connell 2021: 228).

women, like other female animals, naturally tend to be gentle, intelligent, and lacking in spirit.

3.3 Spirit versus Intelligence or a Balance of the Two?

In Aristotelian zoology an animal is normally either (1) spirited, wild, and ferocious or (2) intelligent, gentle, and friendly (and so can become tame). In his *Politics*, Aristotle attempts to combine (1) and (2) within the same individual. This may be what brings him to make a special case for human blood as facilitating both boldness and intelligence.

> The best [animals] have hot, thin and pure [blood]. For such animals are at the same time well-endowed with respect to courage and intelligence (*phronēsis*). (*PA* 2.2.648a9–11)

The idea seems to be that boldness will come from the heat and intelligence from the purity of the blood. But this does not really work since without an earthy, thick element in it (i.e. fibres), spirit will be ineffectual (650b21–3). The thought that it is difficult for an individual to have a bodily constitution that supports the utmost intelligence and the utmost aggression is present in many other writings. For example, the pseudo-Aristotelian *Physiognomics* has it that 'compassion goes with wisdom and cowardice, hardness of heart with stupidity and effrontery' (*Phgn.* 3.808b1). Plato, who also prizes those who are both intelligent and aggressive, notes that this combination is extremely rare given that warriors are usually dim witted and have difficulty learning (*Rep.* 503d1–3).[54] This idea is evident also in Aristotle's ethical works where, for example, the young are too hot-tempered, impetuous, and unthinking to do moral philosophy (*EN* 1.3.1095a3–7).

Aristotle insists that those in the best locality have an ideal natural temperament when they are both spirited and intelligent (*Pol.* 7.6.1327b30–31). While it seemed that intelligence went along with a mild or gentle temperament, Aristotle notes that spirit can also be the origin of affectionate tendencies:

> *Thumos* is the quality of the soul which begets friendship and enables us to love; notably the spirit within us is more stirred against our friends. (*Pol.* 7.7.1327b37–1328a1)[55]

In this context, Aristotle sees spirit as the basis for friendship, despite aggressive and spirited natures sitting on the opposite scale to the mild and gentle ones in his zoology. If the thumetic soul is the source of all feelings or emotional

---

[54] Plato attempts to combine both qualities in his ideal rulers. See, for example, *Rep.* 6.486b–c; 6.503d–e; 7.535b–d.

[55] All translations of *Pol.* 7–8 are from Kraut (1997).

capacities, it makes sense to see it as the source of affection. Even in the non-human context, there may be reason to connect spiritedness with affection in the sense that strong ties of affection can elicit aggressive or angry responses. There is a hint of this in the zoological passage we have just considered where the more spirited male cephalopod is a 'readier ally' (*boēthētikōteron, HA* 8.1.608b16).

The biological works offer some help in finding a way to combine intelligence and spirit, although this does not support any clear gender divide on the matter. In the zoology, two different scales appear to be in play – from mildness to anger1 (or wildness) and from fear to anger2 (or proto-courage). Spirit is the origin of both scales. Aristotle suggests that untamed animals are simply wild and not courageous; they combine anger1 with fear.

> For neither in lower animals nor in the case of foreign types do we see that courage goes with the wildest, but rather with the gentler and lion-like temperaments (*Pol.* 8.2.1338b16–18).

In cases such as these, these animals (and foreign humans) have anger1 instead of mild spirit and lack spirit (anger2) on the scale to do with fear – so they are wild and full of fear (one explanation of animal spirit is closely connected to their fear of those they perceive to be threatening).

The aim is for spirit (i.e. anger2) to be extreme on the scale away from fear, but for mildness (and lack of aggressive spirit) to be combined with that. For example, the lion that is fierce but tameable.[56]

> For even the lion, although it is very dangerous when feeding, if it is not hungry and has fed is very gentle (*praotatos*). In character it is not shy nor suspicious of anything, and towards those reared with it and familiar it is very playful and affectionate. (*HA* 8.43.629b8–12)

Thus, spirit is thought of here as the natural source of mildness combined with proto-courage (or anger2), as in the tamed lion. This idea also allows Aristotle to explain why regimes that focus on harsh physical exercises for the young do not really teach courage but only 'wildness' (*Pol.* 8.2.1338b11–14).

However, this mild spirit is not something that females lack; rather, they lack the 'wild' spirit. Within Aristotle's account of animal character, female Laconian dogs are better formed by nature than their male counterparts (*HA* 8.1.608a25–33). Both male and female dogs are said to be courageous. They combine tamed mildness and a lack of fear, which allows for something closer to courage than mere automatic aggression sparked by fear. Furthermore, it is female animals who display behaviours in the natural cycles of reproduction

---

[56] For a lion-like physiognomy as a 'sign' of courage see *Phgn.* 1.805b25; 5.809b15–36.

that more closely resemble mild spirit (i.e. anger1). They hit out at aggressors not out of fear but to protect their own, most often their offspring (e.g. *HA* 6.18.571b29–30). Aristotle's definition of anger (which I take to be derived from anger2) in the *Rhetoric* mentions care for others (*Rh.* 2.2.1378a30–2); anger includes 'apparent insult' to 'one's own', that is, one's family and friends. Despite the prominence of care for others in what motivates anger, most accounts of emotions in Aristotle's work focus on the individual and their desire for self-assertion.[57] The spirit in female animals manifests itself in a strength to love and protect those loved ones. Thus, the female character from the *HA* can be seen to support a better-spirited attitude in females than in males and does not preclude them from experiencing strong affection.[58]

3.4 Do Men and Women Complement Each Other?

The role of warrior and counsellor (*bouleutikos*) are assigned to the same people at different stages of their life, since younger men are physically stronger and older men are wiser (*Pol.* 7.9.1329a5–16).[59] This, Aristotle says, is an 'order prescribed by nature' (a14). Some scholars propose that Aristotle thinks of the 'natural' differences between men and women in a similar way. By way of comparison, in Plato's *Politicus* two different tendencies in the citizens must balance each other out. The naturally courageous tend to be excessively aggressive and are swift to act, while the naturally moderate are overly slow and cautious. For Plato, these are two different types of men, but the idea that they may be joined in a 'unified social structure' (*Politicus* 307d6–309b4) could be applied to the way that men and women balance each other's tendencies and compensate for each other's deficiencies.[60]

There is some attraction in this scheme. But it fails to adequately capture Aristotle's account of men's control over women. The slight differences in the character tendencies of typical men and women mean that men overpower

---

[57] This emphasis on self-assertion partly has to do with the continuity between Homeric ideas of honour. See Harris (2001: ch.1).

[58] '[A]lthough lack of spirit does not seem to prevent women from forming friendships … these relations may not extend beyond the members of the household so as to include communal friendships. Lack of spirit thus seems to hold back women from performing the kinds of actions and forming the kinds of bonds that are constitutive of the political, virtuous life' (Leunissen 2017: 160). Aristotle never says that women do not form friendships outside of their household. Furthermore, the bonds with family members are stronger than those of their husbands (to be discussed in Section 5).

[59] Plato's *Rep.* recommends warlike activities for the younger guardians and more intellectual pursuits as they age.

[60] Dodds argues that men's spiritedness and women's nurturance complement each other in the family and community (1996: 82–87). See also Lockwood (2003: 10–11).

women, but because women are human, free, intelligent, and ought to be virtuous and happy, balance is not the right way to characterise this situation.

4 The Ethical Woman

Aristotle is clear that in order be able to become good (*agathos*) and decent (*spoudaios*), one must be born human (*Pol.* 7.12.1332a40–41). He adds that it is necessary to have a certain sort (*poion*) of body and soul (1332b1–3). Whether being born a woman hampers moral development requires further investigation. This section will consider in an ethical context the infamous Aristotelian idea that women's deliberative faculty lacks authority. Women's capacity to achieve the canonical virtues of courage and (practical) wisdom will be set out in an Aristotelian framework and in the context of citizen marriage. Given my earlier account of Aristotle's view of the capacities that women have, the claim that they are intellectually and/or morally impaired is undermined.[61]

4.1 *Akuros* in Context: Marital Rule

Aristotle's account of politics begins with a basic human connection – that between a man and a woman when they come together to begin a genetic family:

> Now in this as in other fields we shall get the best view of things if we look at their natural growth from their beginnings. First, those which are incapable of existing without each other must unite as a pair. For example, male and female, for generation (and this not from choice; rather, as in other animals too and in plants, the urge to leave behind another such as oneself is natural). (*Pol.* 1.1.1252a24–30)[62]

The pairing of men and women is not driven by sexual desire but by a natural urge to generate another.[63] Aristotle's focus is on marriage between citizens that will produce legitimate citizen children (*Pol.* 3.2.1275b22–3).[64] The citizens are neither slaves nor disenfranchised workers such as farmers, miners, sailors, or craftspeople.[65] Citizens have the capacity for happiness due to both political

---

[61] For intellectual impairment see especially Leunissen (2017: 154–5); Karbowski (2012, 2014a, 2014b); Riesbeck (2015); Kraut (1997: 107). The supposed physiological basis for this has been addressed and challenged in Section 2. For moral without intellectual impairment see Fortenbaugh (1977); Nielsen (2015).

[62] All translations of *Pol.* 1–2 are from Saunders (1995) (sometimes modified).

[63] *DA* 2.4.415a26–b7. Human being is a 'household animal' (*EE* 7.10.1242a24) and is 'by nature a pairing thing more than a political thing' (*EN* 8.13.1162a17). See also Xenophon *Mem.* 2.2.4: 'Of course you don't suppose that lust provokes people to beget children'.

[64] Aristotle recognises the desire to have genetic children (*Pol.* 2.1.1262a2–24).

[65] Aristotle tells approvingly of a policy in Thebes whereby trading in the marketplace disqualified a person from office for ten years (*Pol.* 3.5.1278a25–7).

engagement and leisure (1275a22–3).[66] Citizens choose who they have children with and how to bring about these children (*Pol.* 7.10.1242a24).[67]

The power relationship (literally the relation of ruling and being ruled) between a man and a woman exemplifies or mimics a basic power relation in the city: 'marital' rule (*gamikē*: an Aristotelian coinage)[68] is 'political', meaning that it is rule between equals.

> A husband and father, we saw, rules over wife and children, both free, but the rule differs, the rule over his children is kingly, over his wife political rule. For although there may be exceptions to the order of nature, the male is by nature fitter for command than the female, just as the elder and full-grown is superior to the younger and more immature. But in the most political states the citizens rule and are ruled by turns, for the idea of a political state implies that the natures of the citizens are equal, and do not differ at all. (*Pol.* 1.12.1259a38–b5)

Aristotle is keen to differentiate marital rule from the type of rule that exists in the case of master and slave and parent and child. He characterises the slave as the property of the master (*Pol.* 1.4) and the child as a part of the parent, and is quite clear that women are neither a part nor property of their husbands (1.7.1255b16–20; 3.6.1278b30–40).[69] The wife is not a slave, as he repeatedly emphasises.[70] If women are separate free persons, why are they under the perpetual rule of their husbands?

Aristotle gives what appears to be a 'natural' rationale:

> Most instances of ruling and being ruled are natural. For rule of free over slave, male over female, man over child, is exercised in different ways, because, while the parts of the soul are present in all of them, they are present in them in different ways. The slave is completely without the deliberative capacity; that female has it, but it has no authority (*akuros*); the child has it, but undeveloped. (*Pol.* 1.13.1260a8–14)

The most popular way to understand '*akuros*'[71] focuses on women's psychological state. Women are deemed to be 'constitutionally akratic'[72] with respect to pleasure and the avoidance of pain.

---

[66] Obviously, women did not have direct political participation; it seems that they count as citizens in some relaxed sense as members of the relevant community. See footnote 8.

[67] Pellegrin (2015: 43).   [68] Riesbeck (2015: 134).

[69] Deslauriers (2015: 59); Riesbeck (2015: 134).

[70] Deslauriers (2015: 48). In *Pol.* 1.1.1252b1, Aristotle oddly phrases this as female and slave being distinct, even though there were female slaves. See also *Pol.* 1.1.1252a7–16. Reisbeck (2015: 134).

[71] As Scott remarks, 'he does not seem at all interested in developing the point' (2010: 112). For Riesbeck (2015: 140), it is 'obscure', complicating even further the distinction in rule it was meant to clarify.

[72] Modrak (1994: 213).

4.2 Women as Akratic

Aristotle says that females are 'softer' (*malakōteron*) than males in the *HA* (8.1.608a25–6; 608b1) and he uses the term 'soft' (*malakos*) for a certain type of ethical weakness in the *Nicomachean Ethics*.[73]

> Someone who is deficient in withstanding what most people withstand, and are capable of withstanding, is soft (*malakos*) and self-indulgent; for self-indulgence is a kind of softness. This person trails his cloak to avoid the labour and pain of lifting it, and imitates an invalid. (*EN* 7.7.1150b1–5)[74]

The trope of the trailed cloak features in many narratives about effeminate foreigners (e.g. *Pol.* 1311b40ff.). The female is mentioned shortly after this passage:

> It is surprising if someone is overcome by what most people can resist, and is incapable of withstanding it, unless due to the nature of the type or because of disease – as, e.g., the Scythian kings' softness because of the race, and as the female is distinguished from the male. (1150b13–16)

The association between softness and the female leads some commentators to the generalisation that all women (or even all females) 'are less able to endure pain and hardships and to do without certain comforts than males' (Mayhew 2004: 99).[75]

For Aristotle, the akratic generates correct judgements but regularly acts against these due to 'strong feelings' (7.3.1147a14–15).[76] The 'simple' or soft akratic is concerned with pleasure and pain (7.4.1147b23–5).

> Some of these people go to excess in pursuing these pleasant things and avoiding painful things – hunger, thirst, heat, cold and all that concerns touch and taste – not, however, because they have decided on it, but in conflict with their decision and thought. (7.4.1148a6–10)

This state is described as being akratic about 'appetites' (*epithumiai*). Aristotle contrasts it with *akrasia* about 'spirit' (*thumos*). We have already learned in the last section that women (and many other female animals) are less spirited than males; this means they are less prone to *akrasia* about spirit. Due to the

---

[73] Quoting *Historia Animalium* 8.1 extensively, Nielsen remarks: 'The passage confirms Aristotle's observation in *Nicomachean Ethics* 7.7 that the female is distinguished from the male by softness' (2015: 579). See also the discussion in Mayhew (2004: 98–9) and Leunissen (2017: 157–61).

[74] All translations of *EN* are from Irwin (1985) (sometimes modified).

[75] See also Fortenbaugh (1977); Smith (1983); Modrak (1994); Karbowski (2012); Nielsen (2015); Riesbeck (2015); Leunissen (2017: ch. 6), and Harris (2001: 272) for this view.

[76] Akratics do not abide by their decisions (*EN* 7.1.1145b11–12; 7.9.1151a29–33; 7.10.1152a18–19).

sensitivity of their bodies, they are more likely to be prone to *akrasia* about pleasure and pain.

Many commentators associate the congenital *akrasia* of all females in Aristotle both with the simple or soft variety and with the 'impetuous' sort detailed in the following passage.[77]

> One type of *akrasia* is impetuosity (*propeteia*), while another is weakness (*astheneia*). For the weak person deliberates, but then his feeling makes him abandon the result of his deliberation; but the impetuous person is led on by his feelings because he has not deliberated . . . . Quick-tempered and melancholic people are most prone to be impetuous akratics. For in quick-tempered people the appetite is so fast, and in melancholic people so intense, that they do not wait for reason, because they tend to follow appearance. (*EN* 7.7.1150b19–28)

'Quick-tempered' is sometimes translated as 'irascible' and associated with women. This is not, however, a term Aristotle uses to describe women in the *HA* or anywhere.[78] The impetuous akratic is more likely to be led by spirit rather than appetitive desire, displaying a more masculine sort of weakness.[79] Quick-tempered people, led by spirit, fly into a rage at everything (*EN* 5.4.1126a18–19). The description of feminine despondency in the *HA* fits much better to 'bitter people' (*hoi pikroi*) who are angry for a long time because they cannot exact revenge easily (*EN* 5.5.1126a20–27). Thus, to lump together irascibility with general 'lack of self-control' as 'effeminate' is inaccurate.[80]

The more masculine *akrasia* about spirit is viewed in a more positive light by Aristotle than *akrasia* about appetites. First of all, it is not 'scheming':

> Moreover, those who plot more are more unjust. But the spirited person does not plot (*epiboulos*), and neither does spirit; it is open (*phaneros*). Lower appetite (*epithumia*), however, is like what they say about Aphrodite, 'trick-weaving Cypris', and what Homer says about her embroidered girdle: 'Blandishment, which steals the wits even of the very intelligent'. (*EN* 7.7.1149b13–18)

---

[77] Nielsen (2015: 578): 'Either she impetuously flees or shrinks back in the face of danger, not pausing to deliberate (call this "impetuous softness"), or she does pause to deliberate, and reaches the right decision, but is subsequently overwhelmed by feelings of fear such that she abandons the decision once made ("weak softness"). According to Aristotle, then, women either fail to consider their convictions or they lack the courage of their convictions'.

[78] Karbowski (2014b: 99). Aristotle does not say that female animals suffer from *propeteia* (impetuousness) in the *Historia Animalium*, but this seems anomalous.

[79] Other than melancholics, the only example Aristotle gives of impetuous appetitive *akrasia* is the sweet eater (*EN* 7.3).

[80] See, for example, Dutsch and Konstan (2011: 59).

We might infer from this that any person who succumbs to a weakness for bodily pleasures is in a much more complicated mental state. The lower appetites exact some kind of control over reason.[81] The reference to Aphrodite suggests the stereotype of female sexual voracity. It is, however, striking that the quotation comes from a female intellectual, Sappho, who is at least able to reflect on this weakness. Furthermore, the second quotation from Homer has Aphrodite lending her girdle to Hera in order to distract her husband with sexual desire (*Iliad* 14.214–23). And so this is not an instance of *a woman* who is overcome by appetite for sexual love but a male god, Zeus.

Although women may be constitutionally more prone to *akrasia* due to lower appetites, for Aristotle, there are many men who are also prone to this ethical weakness.[82] Furthermore, while noting that 'natural' *akrasia* is more difficult to overcome (*EN* 7.10.1152a29–31), Aristotle is not deterministic about these tendencies.[83] The only person who is 'incurable' is the one with 'no regrets' (7.7.1150a21–2); this would not be an akratic person in any case, since *akrasia* involves the realisation of the mistake and subsequent recovery of correct judgement (7.3.1147b6–8).[84] Fortenbaugh (1977: 138–9) uses the case of Medea to support the view that all women are akratic. Medea is aware of her own condition: 'I know well what awful harm I am about to inflict, but my passionate rage (*thumos*) overbears my thinking (*bouleumatōn*)' (Eur. *Med.* 1078–80). This means she is not incurable. In any case, as her *akrasia* is not the usual feminine variety, she cannot be used as a case study for female moral psychology.

Given that all humans can resist nature through habit and reason,[85] the most that can be established on the basis of these passages is that women are more prone to a certain moral weakness and not that they inevitably suffer from it. For those who opt for the intrapersonal reading of *akuros* in the famous passage at 1260a13, therefore, the fact that *akrasia* is curable is problematic.[86] If the claim has to do with the state of a woman's psyche, then once this has been ameliorated, she will not have an *akuros* deliberative faculty and so there will be no

---

[81] See also *EN* 7.10.1152a18–19, where the weak akratic is likened to a 'plotter'. Nielsen (2015: 579) thinks that for Aristotle 'Female duplicity would seem to be grounded partly in keener intelligence'.

[82] Aristotle only ever discusses male appetitive *akrasia* in his ethics (Riesbeck 2015: 143 n.33). The comment at *Pol.* 1.1.1253a36–8, that when without virtue humans are the most unscrupulous and savage of animals, notes appetitive *akrasia* (sexual indulgence and gluttony) and applies it to men and women equally.

[83] Swanson (1992: 67).   [84] The akratic 'notices' that they are akratic (7.1.1145b11; 1150b36).

[85] *Pol.* 7.13.1332a39–b8; *EN* 1.1.1214a19–21.

[86] Riesbeck (2015: 144–5) posits that women are curable through education. 'Aristotle's claim need not be understood to be that *akrasia* is inevitable in women, but that marital rule is precisely what enables women to overcome this natural deficiency'.

reason to exclude her from rule.[87] This difficulty leads some to posit that for Aristotle women's intellectual capacities must be defective in a way that makes it impossible for them to participate in public life.[88] Rather than suggesting some special mental infirmity in women, the difficulty of excluding them from politics in Aristotle's view, shows up tensions in his thought about their role in the city.[89]

There are other reasons to resist the intrapersonal reading. First of all, citizen wives are in charge of the household, including such tasks as cooking, weaving, nursing, and supervising servants.[90] If they really were chronically akratic, it would be very difficult, if not impossible, for them to carry out these extensive duties.[91] Another strike against this viewpoint is that it is very difficult to combine with Aristotle's advocacy of general happiness and virtue.[92] At *Pol.* 7.13.1331b40–1332a1, Aristotle mentions that some people will have only a small share in happiness due to 'some accident or defect of nature'. He does not specify who these people are; some conclude he means to indicate women. But other evidence points towards Aristotle advocating the virtues and happiness of women.[93]

4.3 The Nature of Female Virtue

Aristotle considers women's virtue to be similar enough to men's to be the basis for character friendship that is of 'good people similar in virtue' (*EN* 8.3.1156b6–7). There are, for Aristotle, three varieties of friendship (8.2.1156a4–6). The two lesser types can develop into complete friendship if the friends are both good and begin to base their friendship on character rather than pleasure or utility (8.4.1157a11–14). Marriage is a case in point.

> The friendship between husband and wife seems to exist according to nature. For a human is more by nature a coupling (*sunduastikon*) than a political (*politikon*) being, in as much as the household is more necessary than the

---

[87] Scott (2010: 115): 'if the disconnect has been repaired, why can women not take the highest offices in the state?' See also Riesbeck (2015: 149 and references in note 52); Nichols (1987); Levy (1990: 403). Karbowski sees this as a problem for Fortenbaugh's interpretation; he attempts to 'solve' it by positing an intrinsic psychological deficiency in women that makes them capable only of household tasks. On this reading, nature makes them this way for the sake of the *polis* (2012, 2014b; for a critique see Section 3.3).

[88] Karbowski (2014b: 97–8).   [89] Levy (1990: 400–401). See Section 5.

[90] For references, see Karbowski (2014a: 454) (Xenophon *Oec.* 7.35–37; 41–42). See also *Lysias* I.

[91] Deslauriers (2003: 223). See also Scott (2010: 114–15); Frede (2019: 264).

[92] *Pol.* 1.13.1259b36–1260a1; *EN* 8.7.1162a22–8; *Rh.* 1.5.1361a11–12.

[93] Aristotle says that children and animals cannot be happy but does not include women on that list (*EN* 1.9.1099b33–1100a4).

polis, and producing children more common amongst animals. Whereas in other animals the sharing extends to this, human beings don't only live together in order to produce young but also for the sake of their 'way of life' (*bios*). For straightaway the tasks/works are divided, and husband and wife are different. They provide for each other, their particular talents being put towards what is common. Because of these things, there seems to be utility and pleasure in their friendship. It can also be due to virtue, if they are good (*epieikeis*).[94] For there is a virtue of each, and they may rejoice in that. Children seem to be a bond, for which reason couples without children separate more. For children are a good common to both, and the common holds together. (8.12.1162a16–33, my translation)

The lifelong commitment of marriage is one that builds on 'experience' and 'becoming accustomed' to one another (8.3.1156b25–6; 8.6.1158a15–16). Another aspect of the friendship of two decent people, which the ideal marriage is supposed to be, is that each approves of and corrects the other (8.12.1172a10–12).[95]

[F]riendly feeling consists in equality and similarity, especially the similarity of those who are alike in virtue; for being true to themselves, these also remain true to one another, and neither request nor render services that are morally degrading. Indeed they may be said actually to restrain each other from evil; since good people neither err themselves nor permit their friends to err. (8.8.1159b2–7).

The way in which close friendship for Aristotle challenges autonomy has been noted by many scholars.[96] Friends such as these share perception and understanding (*EE* 7.12.1245a5–10). The virtues of good husbands and wives must be close enough for this interconnected human relation, making a joint and collaborative effort to achieve their objectives.[97]

To have the same goals means having the same 'vision of how to attain the human good'.[98]

---

[94] While this term does not immediately suggest practical wisdom, *phronēsis*, it is one that Aristotle uses of the most exalted virtues in his ethics, including at *EN* 4.9.1128b21, where it is used of those who are uninterruptedly capable of acting correctly, and at *EN* 4.7.1127b3, where it is associated with being entirely committed to the truth. At *EN* 10.5, the *epieikēs* person is one who is able to 'improve the law if it is in need of correction' (1175b24). It is hoped that women can be *spoudaiai* at *Pol.* 1.12.1260b17–18.

[95] Swanson (1992: 52). Swanson claims that the marital relation 'is reciprocal and approaches equality also in that each partner' rectifies flaws in the others (55, citing 1160b33–5; 1162b22–4).

[96] Sherman (1989: ch.6); Connell (2019); Brill (2020, especially ch. 1).

[97] Participants in some sense 'share in joint deliberation about their common activities' (Riesbeck 2015: 134). Another idea is that rulers are 'ruled by' those they rule over insofar as they must take into account their subjects 'desires and opinions' (Nichols 1992: 159). See also the justice of equals in marriage noted at *EN* 5.4.1134b16–18 and by Deslauriers (2015: 47 n.5).

[98] Brill (2020: 64).

> Concord is found in decent people (*tois epieikesin*). For they are in concord
> with themselves and with each other, since they are practically of the same
> mind (*homonoous*); for their wishes are stable, not flowing back and forth like
> a tidal strait. They wish for what is just and advantageous, and also seek it in
> common. (9.9.1167b4–9)

There is a complication for this picture, however, which is that friendship
between husband and wife is unequal.

> But there is a different kind of friendship, which involves superiority of one
> party over the other, for example, the friendship between father and son, and
> generally between an older person and a younger, and that between husband
> and wife, and between any ruler and the person ruled. (8.7.1158b11–14)

Since virtue friendship is based on 'equality' (8.7.1157b35–1158a1) how can
husband and wife have this connection? Aristotle explains as follows: friendship of husband for wife is not same as wife for husband, 'for each of these
persons has a different virtue and function, and also different motive for their
regard, and so the affection and friendship they feel are different' (8.7.1158b17–
20). When one person is superior to the other, the friendship is 'equalised' by the
lesser individual loving the superior one more (1158b26).[99] '[T]he better party
receives a larger share [of good], while each party receives what is appropriate
to each' (8.11.1161a24–5).

    The difference between ruler and ruled over in the household grounds their
differences in virtue. While 'the ruler', the husband, has complete virtue of
character, the wife has a virtue 'proper' to her (*Pol.* 1.12.1260a18–20).

> Clearly, then, moral virtue belongs to all of them [that is, rulers and subjects];
> but the temperance of a man and of a woman, or the courage and justice of
> a man and of a woman, are not, as Socrates maintained, the same; the courage
> of a man is as ruling, of a women is as assistant (*hupēretikē*). And this holds of
> all other virtues. (*Pol.* 1.12.1260a20–24)

The term translated 'assistant', *hupēretikē,* derives from rowers of a trireme.
Some see this as the mere virtue of obeying, but it can be read in a much less
negative light.[100] For one thing, Aristotle is not as disparaging about actual
oarsmen.

> Like a sailor, the citizen is a member of a community. Now, sailors have
> different functions, for one of them is a rower (*hē eretēs*), another a pilot, and
> a third a look-out man, a fourth is described by some similar term; and while
> the precise definition of each individual's virtue applies exclusively to him,

---

[99] 'For when the love is in proportion to the merit of the parties, then in a sense arises equality'.
[100] The text does not say that the virtue of a woman is in 'obeying', which most take it to
(Deslauriers 2003: 216; Lockwood 2003: 11; Scott 2010: 107).

there is, at the same time, a common definition applicable to them all. For they have all of them a common object, which is safety in navigation. Similarly one citizen differs from another, but the salvation of the community is the common business of them all. (*Pol.* 3.3.1276b20–29)[101]

This passage suggests that the oarsmen, just as much as pilots, have the general virtue of promoting civic well-being. One can imply that the virtue of helpers, the lesser oarsmen, is also crucial for common goals.

This whole section of the *Politics* emphasises the importance of family friendship in the establishment and continuity of the best communities.

> [T]here arise in cities family connexions, brotherhoods, common sacrifices, amusements which draw people together. But these are created by friendship, for to choose to live together is friendship. The end of the state is the good life, and these are the means towards it. And the state is the union of families and villages in a perfect and self-sufficing life, by which we mean a happy and honourable life. (*Pol.* 3.9.1280b36–1281a2)

In the context of community life, central to happiness, humans assist one another (*EN* 8.8.1159b5; 9.2.1164b25; *EE* 7.2.1237b19). Even the great-souled man (*megalopsuchos*) must assist others (4.3.1124b18).[102] The one who always commands without assisting is a one-sided person who cannot feel the perspective of those he rules over and is bound to rule without understanding.

> There is rule of another kind, which is exercised over freemen and equals by birth – a political rule, which the ruler must learn by being ruled over, as he would learn the duties of a general of cavalry by being under the orders of a general of cavalry, or the duties of a general of infantry by being under the orders of a general of infantry, and by having had the command of a regiment and of a company. It has been well said that he who has never learned to be ruled over cannot be a good commander. (*Pol.* 3.4.1277b7–13)

Those who are under the just leader fully endorse and understand the goals and values at issue. In fact, by being under this command, they understand it better. Thus, if the wife assists then she also endorses the overall good that her sub-decisions within the household achieve for the *polis*, such as the birth and raising of fine citizens for the future.

Women's virtues are auxiliary but still genuine; they are, however, different from those of men. Aristotle says that 'those who enumerate the virtues of different persons separately, as Gorgias does are much more correct' than those

---

[101] All translations of *Pol.* 3 are from Solomon (Aristotle 1984a).

[102] While Riesbeck acknowledges the scope of the idea of assistance in Aristotelian ethics, he does not apply this to wives (2015: 151 n.56).

that give a general account (*Pol.* 1.13.1260a27–8). However, his own position ends up much further away from Gorgias's view than this comment suggests.[103] For Gorgias virtue, *aretē*, is performing a certain assigned task well. The virtue of a knife is to cut well; the virtue of a wife is 'ordering the house well, preserving the things inside, and being obedient (*katēkoon*) to her husband' (Plato, *Meno* 71e8–9). For Aristotle, virtue is not the performing of an assigned task well; it is the operation of the general human capacity for practical wisdom.

> Virtue, then, is a state that decides (*prohairetikē*), [consisting] in a mean, the mean relative to us, which is defined by reference to reason, i.e., to the reason by reference to which the intelligent person (*ho phronimos*) would define it. (*EN* 2.6.1006b37–1107a3)

The reasoning involved in virtue is not supposed to be the reasoning involved in reaching a goal set for a person. Instead, Aristotelian virtues are general dispositions such as courage and temperance (*Pol.* 7.1.1323a27–9).

One key problem with understanding what Aristotle means concerning women's virtues is that he switches between saying that such virtues differ in kind (*Pol.* 1.12.1259b36–8) and that they differ in degree (1.12.1260a16–19; 3.4.1277a20–b25). The latter idea is problematic; 'virtue' does not seem to be something that you can have a little of.[104] It makes sense, then, to think that when talking in terms of degrees, he is slipping into common parlance to appeal to the more general audience.[105] His more considered view is that the virtues of men and women differ according to their activities and the objects they deal with.[106] In an attempt to elucidate this, we will consider how courage and practical wisdom could apply to women's activities for Aristotle.

4.3.1 Courage

Aristotle explicitly gives men and women different roles with respect to the household at *Politics* 3.2.1277b24–5: the man procures and the woman preserves (*phulattein*). He doesn't link this to differing emotional tendencies, but others have suggested that, in line with Xenophon's *Oeconomicus*, Aristotle imagines that the more timid and fearful nature of women makes them suited to

---

[103] Scott (2010: 101).

[104] Scott also notices this problem (2010: 119 n.41). Also Stauffner (2008: 938). Dodds is adamant that the virtues of men and women are equal in value for Aristotle (1996: 78).

[105] Appealing to the views of common people, Aristotle writes: 'virtuous actions are nobler when they proceed from those who are naturally worthier, for example, from a man rather than a woman' (*Rh.* 1.9.1367a17–19; Cf. *Poet.* 15.1454a16–31).

[106] In the friendship of husband and wife, one must consider that 'for each of these persons has a different virtue and function' (*EN* 8.7.1158b17–18).

preserving the household goods.[107] In *Rhetoric* 2.5.1383a6–7, Aristotle notes an important connection between fear and deliberation. 'Fear sets us thinking what can be done (*ho phobos bouleutikous poiei*)'. While the fearful (and thoughtful) tendencies in women might be useful, when viewed in contradistinction to men's courage these attributes look to indicate a lack of courage. There is one area of life, however, where women would have required courage: giving birth. In classical Greece, a married woman would have been expected to have children (*Pol.* 7.16; cf. *HA* 5.14.545b27–31; 9.6.585b6–7). Aristotle is aware of the high rate of infant mortality, referring to it several times (*Pol.* 2.6.1265b7–8; *EN* 1.8.1099b2–6; *HA* 9.8.588a8–10).[108] In order to ensure that a family has two healthy children, a woman would have had to go through around ten births. In pre-industrial societies maternal mortality is staggeringly high.[109] Many complications in birth, including mis-presentation, foetal death, and failure of placental expulsion, are recorded in the fourth century Hippocratic *Diseases of Women*. Other than a few primitive procedures, there is no indication that Hippocratic medicine would have greatly improved a woman's chances; indeed, the interventions recommended in the absence of antiseptic procedures were likely to have resulted in infection and death. Ensuring a healthy next generation was risky for any woman, including the citizen wife. Indeed, Aristotle notes that both pregnancy and childbirth are much more difficult for sedentary citizen women (*GA* 4.6.775a22–b2; *HA* 9.9.586b35–587a5).[110]

The idea that childbirth requires something equivalent in women to masculine courage was certainly available in ancient Greece. The most striking statement comes from Euripides' *Medea*.

> Men say that we live a life free from danger at home while they fight with the spear. How wrong they are! I would rather stand three times with a shield in battle than give birth once. (248–51, trans. Kovacs)

---

[107] Xenophon (*Oec.* 7.22–5); Riesbeck (2015: 148).

[108] Kraut's estimate of a mortality rate of 25–35 per cent during the first year is too low. His view that Aristotle addresses this problem adequately by suggesting some physical exercise seems overly optimistic (1997: 80).

[109] Maternal mortality in today's developing countries is an important source of information, given that the lack of access to modern medicine is similar to the ancient world. In Southern Sudan in 2017, there was 1 maternal death per 100 births (www.who.int/news-room/fact-sheets/detail/maternal-mortality). The lifetime risk of maternal death in rural Africa is 1 in 26. A common saying in these parts is 'a pregnant women has one foot in the grave' and euphemisms are used prior to childbirth such as 'I am going to the river to fetch some water; it is so very treacherous; I may not come back' (Lewis 2008).

[110] The uncertainty of healthy children (and surviving gravidae) is evident in huge reproductive anxiety in the literature of ancient Greece. See Cole (2004, ch.5). The situation was not much different for elite women in seventeenth- and eighteenth-century England. Queen Anne, who married at age eighteen, had seventeen pregnancies but only five live births (Gregg 2001).

Another indication that the dangers of giving birth were acknowledged comes from Plutarch's account of Sparta's medals for mothers.[111] Xenophon joins in with his description of Socrates' defence of Xanthippe to their son:

> The woman conceives and bears her burden in travail, risking her life, and giving of her food; and, with much labour, having endured to the end and brought forth her child, she rears and cares for it, although she has not received any good thing; and the babe neither recognises its benefactress nor can make its wants known to her. (*Mem.* 2.2.5–6, trans. Marchant)

In this exclusive sphere of womanly activity, courage was required.[112] The good the woman receives is not from the child itself but from the knowledge that she is acting in an exemplary fashion when risking her own life.

Let's consider whether facing death in childbirth or shortly thereafter would count as courage for Aristotle. Aristotle defines courage as follows.

> Standing firm against what is painful makes us call people courageous; that is why courage is both painful and justly praised, since it is harder to stand firm against something painful than to refrain from something pleasant. (*EN* 3.9.1117a33–365)

Aristotle associates courage with facing death, but not in all situations.

> Then what sorts of frightening conditions concern the courageous person? Surely the most frightening; for no one stands firmer against terrifying conditions. Now death is the most frightening of all … Still, not even death in all conditions, e.g. on the sea or in sickness, seems to be the courageous person's concern. (3.6.1115a24–9)

Facing death in war displays courage, whereas facing death due to a sea accident or disease does not.

> In what conditions, then, is death his concern? Surely in the finest conditions. Now such deaths are those in war, since they occur in the greatest and finest danger; and this judgment is endorsed by the honours given in cities and by monarchs. Hence someone is called courageous to the fullest extent if he is intrepid in facing a fine death and the immediate dangers that bring death – and this is above all true of the dangers in war. (*EN* 3.6.1115a29–35)

---

[111] On one reading of Plutarch's *Lycurgus*, at Sparta women who died in childbirth, like men who died in war, were *hieroi*, 'sacred' (Plut. *Lyc.* 27.3). See Dillon (2007).

[112] Compare Hilary Mantel's description of the early modern childbed: 'What is a woman's life? Do not think, because she is not a man, she does not fight. The bedchamber is her tilting ground, where she shows her colours, and her theatre of war is the sealed room where she gives birth. She knows she may not come alive out of that bloody chamber' (2020: 507).

Giving birth to the next generation of citizens is more like war than like accident or illness. It requires more control than being thrown overboard and is non-pathological.

Although Aristotle only mentions death in combat, he leaves room for other ways of facing death to count as courageous.

> Now the courageous person is unperturbed, as far as a human being can be. Hence, though he will fear even the sorts of things that are not irresistible, he will stand firm against them, in the right way, as prescribed by reason, for the sake of what is fine, since this is the end aimed at by virtue. (3.7.1115b10–13)

In giving birth, a process controlled to some extent by attitude and effort, at least as much as action on the battlefield, women are aiming at what is fine. While one might think that women had no choice, this is equally the case of men who were obliged to fight. Furthermore, a woman in these situations will often be experienced, having gone through failed births numerous times before; in this respect she is similar to a hardened warrior.[113]

Staying strong and courageous during the process of giving birth (without modern anaesthesia) does not appear to be something that the 'soft' person does. Also, if a woman dies while giving birth, she knows the value of her action on behalf of the next generation. Given the enormous risks involved in bearing children, one could imagine the following being applied not only to men in Greek societies but also to women:

> Besides, it is true, as they say, that the virtuous person labours for his/her friends and for his/her native country, and will die for them if he/she must; he/she will sacrifice money, honour and contested goods in general, in achieving what is fine for him/herself. (*EN* 9.8.1169a18–22)

4.3.2 Practical Wisdom (Phronēsis)

Full human virtue is only possible with *phronēsis* (*EN* 6.13.1144b31–3); this is the *eudaimōn* (happy) life (3.2.1111b26–9; 3.3.1113a2–5; 6.2.1139a31–b5).[114] If the deliberation that goes on internally to determine the best course of action is not possible at all for women, then neither is virtue or happiness.[115] We have seen how that conclusion clashes with the several points at which Aristotle

---

[113] On the importance of experience for virtue see *EN* 6.8.1142a12–15.

[114] 'Let us agree, then, that each person has just as much happiness as he has virtue and wisdom and action in accordance with them' (*Pol.* 7.1.1323b21–3).

[115] The exact way in which deliberation operates is contested. See especially Nielsen (2011) and Callard (2021).

allows for both in women.[116] For example, he is concerned for the happiness of both (free) men and (free) women at *Pol.* 1.12.1260b19–20. But even if women are not akratic, this doesn't guarantee that they have *phronēsis*.

One passage in the *Politics* present the strongest case for women not having *phronēsis*; it says that this intellectual virtue is not available to anyone who is not a ruler.

> *Phronēsis* is the only virtue peculiar to the ruler: it would seem that all other virtues must equally belong to ruler and subject. The virtue of the subject is certainly not *phronēsis*, but only true opinion (*doxa alēthēs*). (3.4.1277b25–9)

Some conclude from this that since women cannot control external situations through political engagement, they cannot have *phronēsis*. This leads commentators to attribute only 'true opinion' (1277b29) or 'understanding' (*sunēsis*) to wives.[117] Understanding cannot decide but can approve the decisions of others, thus women are able to make sense of and approve the decisions of their husbands. But if Aristotle really thought that women cannot have *phronēsis* then why did he need to mention female virtue? Theirs would simply be an extension of male virtue, just like a slave who undertakes their task in relation to the master (*Pol.* 1.6.1255b11). As several thinkers have pointed out, the husband doesn't stand over and give instructions but delegates whole domains (those 'suited to women', *EN* 8.10.1160b32–5) to his wife for her to deal with on her own.[118] This means that there must be room for citizen women to have *phronēsis* over their own sphere, particularly the home and its maintenance.[119]

Another possible reason for thinking that women cannot have *phronēsis* is that they lack 'practical perception'. This capacity allows individuals to discern the relevant features of their experience in order to make correct decisions (*EN* 2.9.1109b20–23; 4.5.1126a32–b4). If we deny this to women, then it seriously disrupts their envisaged roles and responsibilities within the household that require acute perceptivity of the situation at hand. An experienced mother will

---

[116] 'Since women are not slaves, ... they are not instruments of procreation, and the city is to be designed partly in order to promote their well being' (Kraut 1997: 152). In the *EN* Aristotle insists that happiness will be 'widely shared' (1.9.1099b18–20).

[117] Deslauriers (2015: 61–2).

[118] Nichols (1992: 188 n.37); Dodds (1996: 87); Stauffner (2008: 933–4).

[119] Many commentators note this requirement. For example, Levy (1990: 402): 'a wife could hardly do her work as the ruler in her sphere without her own prudence [i.e. *phronēsis*] in command (*Pol.* 3.4.1277b25ff.)'. Aristotle 'means to attribute to them [i.e. women] the more robust capacity for the active employment to their own practical reasoning' (Riesbeck 2015: 140). See also Saxonhouse (1985: 51); Levy (1990: 405); Mulgan (1994: 187, 198); Dodds (1996: 78–9); Connell (2016: 36–7); Swanson (1992: 56–7). Karbowski posits that women's deliberative faculty isn't unauthoritative; it is literally 'inoperative' (and yet it still operates in the household) (2014a: 456).

recognise what the cry of her child indicates, whether he or she is just fussing or truly distressed and in need of immediate assistance. Arguably, a father with little experience of childcare will not be able to discern such crucial differences in the 'perceptible' particulars.[120] Aristotle is also clear that children benefit most from individualised care and attention; an absent father is much less likely to understand the foibles of each of his infants than a mother who spends most of her days and nights with her charges.[121]

Although many agree that women have *phronēsis* within the home, it is worth challenging the view that their practical intellect is curtailed because of their lack of political involvement. *Phronēsis* is a state of the soul, a disposition, that in many ways does not depend on external circumstances. In order to find out whether participation in politics is actually necessary for complete virtue, it is helpful to consider the context in which the above passage appears. In *Politics* 3, Aristotle is considering a number of questions about what a good citizen is and whether this aligns with being a good person. Along with this, he wonders if citizenship requires someone to 'share in political office' (3.5.1277b34). His conclusions are not dogmatic – different states have different sorts of citizen and in some city-states these do not all have a share in rule. There are also cases in which good people do not correspond to good citizens (3.5.1278a35–1278b5). In this section of the work, then, Aristotle accepts the variety of situations in different states, and it cannot be assumed that he had decided absolutely to place this constraint on virtue for all.[122] Indeed, to fixate on 'share in rule' (i.e. external political power) as necessary for *phronēsis* would put severe limitations on Aristotle's account of the good life, not just for women but for many men as well.[123] According to this reading, *phronēsis* is not possible for those who are not involved in political processes, for example due to a particular

---

[120] Sherman (1989: 154): 'Given her proximity to the children, it is her interactions with them, her clues about what to notice as ethically salient, her instructions about the appropriateness of emotional response and action that are formative. *De facto*, her instructions count for a lot, particularly in a theory which stresses both early development and the special benefits of learning from those whom one loves and trusts'.

[121] While Karbowski doesn't deny that women have this perceptiveness, he speculates that these abilities cannot extend to anything outside the household: 'Aristotle presumably supposes that their practical vision is naturally insensitive to the various demands at the political level' (2014a: 451), maintaining that these are much more complicated. But why would there be any difference between skill in discerning ethical issues in the home as opposed to in the public sphere? Considering Aristotle's great concern for the moral education of children and the harmony of the marital relationship, there is good reason to think that the ethical issues within the home are just as complex as those in the city as a whole. The household is 'a deeply moralized space' (Scott 2020: 205).

[122] The statement occurs in the context of disputing the inclusion of *banausics* (working people) in citizenship and does not say anything about women's part (Samaris 2015).

[123] *Pol.* 3.4.1277b25–6. As Leunissen puts it, 'perhaps even only rulers can possess the virtue of practical wisdom' (2017: 162 n.49).

political system that doesn't broadly distribute power (tyrannies, monarchies, aristocracies, and oligarchies). There is reason to think that *phronēsis* is independent of contingencies such as what type of regime an agent finds themselves subject to. Aristotle notes that although circumstances matter for happiness, virtue is mainly a result of one's own efforts (*EN* 1.9).

> And since it is activities that control life, as we said, no blessed person could ever become miserable, since he will never do hateful and base actions. For a truly good and intelligent persons, we suppose, will bear strokes of fortune suitably, and from his resources at any time will do the finest actions. (1100b33–1101a3)

Rather than requiring control over political circumstances, *phronēsis* looks to be an ability to respond appropriately to the situation one finds oneself in. Despite a lack of political power, women will be able to have rational desires for the good (3.2.1111b26–7; 3.3.1113a2–5; 6.2.1139a31–b5).[124] Deliberation is not mere means–end reasoning but includes a view of the importance of the ends aimed at.[125] As Aristotle puts it:

> It seems proper, then, to an intelligent person (*ho phronimos*) to be able to deliberate finely about what is good and beneficial for himself, not about some restricted area – e.g. about what promotes health and strength – but about what promotes living well in general. (*EN* 6.5.1140a25–8)

What matters most is adhering to the ultimate values that guide one's day to day decisions and the ability to continually reassess these values.[126]

For those who are disenfranchised but who have a deliberative capacity, having a view of the good entails getting behind the values of the society they are a part of and supporting these through their activities where appropriate while attempting to shape those values to the extent that they can. Citizen wives have a vital role to play in both and this seems to be enough to count as a capacity for the Aristotelian *phronēsis* required for the virtuous life. In the marriage relation, although the man has ultimate veto over any decisions about matters affecting the wider community, the wife must be able to sustain her own character.[127] Women are not only receptive to reason, as passive slaves will be,

---

[124] It is worth pointing out that Aristotle uses 'human' (*anthrōpos*) rather than 'man' (*anēr*) to refer to the best individual in the city-state (e.g. *Pol.* 7.3.1325b27, 32; Levy 1990: 398). While he denies that there can be a city of lower animals or slaves, he does not say that there could not be a city of women for the sake of living well (*Pol.* 3.9.1280a31–3). Similarly, he explicitly excludes children and animals from having *phronēsis*, but does not mention women (*EN* 6.13.1144b4–9). If he thought that they were incapable of having it, why wouldn't he have said so?

[125] For an alternative, Humean interpretation of *phronēsis* as means–end reasoning, see Moss (2012).

[126] Wiggins (1975).   [127] Scott (2020: 200–206).

but must also have 'a more robust capacity for the active employment of their own practical reasoning'.[128]

5 The Political Woman

For Aristotle, women can deliberate and stick to their resolutions. This means that their deliberations are not internally ineffective but externally so.[129] This fits the main use of the term *akuros*, which is to specify annulled laws, votes, or decisions.[130] A difficulty for this position is that it leaves Aristotle with no non-circular explanation for the position of women.[131] After detailing Aristotle's recommendations for women's education and their standing as citizen mothers, this section will posit that there is a biological basis for women's subordination.[132] This has to do with their lack of spirit. Despite this shortcoming, citizen women for Aristotle retain an important role in the care and education of children and as possible joint collaborators with their husbands in the goals of the *polis*. Indeed, in some ways, they can be the best of people. The lasting difficulties for Aristotle's insistence on the oppression of women, and how the reference to Sophocles' *Ajax* signals awareness of this, will be touched on in closing.

5.1 Women's Education

In the *Politics* and *Rhetoric* it is noted that, since they constitute half of free people, women must be able to be happy in the good community (*Pol.* 1.13.1260b8–20; 2.9.1269b13–19; *Rh.* 1.5.1361a10–12). It is neglect of this portion of the population that leads to the difficulties that certain regimes experience. One key example is Sparta, where women 'live dissolutely, in respect of every sort of dissoluteness (*akolasia*), and luxuriously (*trupherōs*)' (2.9.1269b22–3). People in Sparta are

---

[128] The quotation is from Riesbeck (2015: 140). Against this view see Karbowski (2014b: 101–3; 2012: 342, 344; 2014a: 436, 457–8), who argues that women have intrinsically 'deficient' rational capacities.

[129] Mulgan (1994); Saxonhouse (1985).

[130] Annulled laws: Plato, *Crito* 50b4; Arist. *EN* 7.9.1151b15–16; *Rh.* 1.15.1376b27; Modrak (1994: 217); Deslauriers (2003: 224); Nielsen (2015: 580–82). Riesbeck (2015: 143–4) places weight on several uses in the biological works (*GA* 4.4.772b27; 4.10.778a1–2; *MA* 2.689b8). In the case of *GA* 4.4.772b27, hermaphrodites are said to have one set of generative organs that are operative and the other that are inoperative, which means that the latter do not work at all and are likened to tumours (*ta phumata*), 'contrary to nature' (*para phusin*). This cannot be the meaning of *akuros* in the *Politics* 1 since women's faculties are not like tumours and cannot be 'contrary to nature'. Scott (2010) takes his meaning of the term from Plato's *Theaetetus* 178d9 and interprets the passage to be saying that women do not have the expertise to pronounce on political matters (112–13).

[131] Riesbeck (2015: 143).

[132] My account is closest to Deslauriers (2015) and Dodds (1996). For clear classification of views that are interpersonal but not conventional, see Riesbeck (2015: 142–3).

under the sway of their women (*gunaikokratoumenoi*) (1269b24–5), leading to a love of wealth (1270a24–5). For Aristotle, the education of children must lead to virtue.[133] Books 7 and 8 of the *Politics*, which provide some guidelines for the '*polis* of our prayers', the best practicable city-state, note that public education will involve gymnastics, music, and literature. In this context, Aristotle talks of two sets of officials, the *paidonomoi* (1336a32) and the *gunakonomoi* – usually translated as 'supervisors of children' and 'supervisors of women'. It is not very clear what exactly these public officials were for, and evidence about the *gunakonomoi* is especially scanty. However, we can find some indication of Aristotle's concern for female education.

The most generally attested role for *gunakonomoi* was arranging religious festivals involving women and girls, for instance selecting those who were to be involved in the Thesmophoria.[134] Philokhoros, a historian who recorded the customs of Attica in the third century, notes that 'the *gunaikonomoi* watched over gatherings in the houses both at weddings and at festivals in general'.[135] In Syracuse, these officers were reported to regulate women's dress in all public contexts and to monitor the nocturnal movements of men as well as women.[136] Their role, then, looks to be one of policing morals, particularly the morals around the decorous behaviour of women in public, marital fidelity, and the suppression of monetary extravagance.[137] The 'supervisor of women' is also mentioned together with the 'supervisor of children' in *Politics* 6, which deals with the pragmatic question of how to improve actual constitutions (6.1.1289a3–7).[138] Perhaps it is no coincidence, then, that the Macedonian politician Demetrius, who was said to have been taught by Theophrastus and perhaps also by Aristotle, strengthened both offices when he took over as *epimelētēs* ('supervisor') of Athens in 318.[139]

By focusing on the role of these officials, and possibly even through his remote influence in the case of Demetrius, one can speculate about what

---

[133] *Pol.* 1.5.1260b16–20.   [134] Lape (2004: 50).

[135] Philokhoros Fragment 65 (Athenaeus, *Deipnosophists* 245c). In a comedy by Menander, the *gunaikonomos* is shown to limit the number of guests allowed at weddings (Lape 2004: 51).

[136] Our source here is Phylarchus, another third century Greek historical writer (*Deipnosophists* 521b, Fragment 45, FGrH 81; Lape 2004: 50). In Syracuse, women were forbidden from wearing gold ornaments, garments embroidered with flowers, and robes with purple borders (Phylarchus Fragment 54: F6H81; Odgen 1996: 370). See also Harding (2008: 168–70).

[137] Odgen (1996: 364–75); Harding (2008: 168–70).

[138] In Smyrna, *paidonomoi* were closely associated with *gunakonomoi*, who were said to be in charge of 'good order (*eukosmia*) and the virgins (*parthenoi*)' (Ogden 1996: 367).

[139] Harding (2008: 169); Lape (2004: 48): 'During his tenure as *epimelētēs*, Demetrius created (or re-created) two magisterial boards, the *nomoplylakes* (guardians of the laws) and the *gynaikonomoi* (the supervisors of women). Taken together, these institutions had broad and unprecedented policing powers, enabling them to intervene in aspects of life not traditionally subject to legislative restraint under the democracy'.

Aristotle thought about the education of citizen women. We already know that he was concerned that if women were not educated toward temperance, they would tend toward being akratic in relation to bodily pleasures. Intemperance is traditionally associated with a love of wealth; this is what Aristotle says led to the love of luxury that was so ruinous in Sparta (2.9.1269b19–1270a12). Thus, laws against extravagance are important for discouraging these tendencies. Marital fidelity is also valued by Aristotle for the usual patriarchal rationale of ensuring one raises one's own genetic offspring.[140]

The ideal role of such officers is likely to have included the early and continued education in the ethical development of girls and young women alongside those officers that concentrated on boys and young men. With respect to girls, Aristotle encourages physical exercise to help with future fertility.

> What qualities should their bodies possess, if they are to be most beneficial to their offspring? This is something to which we must give more attention in our discussion of the upbringing of children, but for now it is enough to speak of it in outline. The condition that athletes are in is not useful for the good condition of a citizen nor for health and procreation, nor is a valetudinarian condition that is quite unfit for work. But the mean between these is useful.[141] Accordingly, one should be in a condition brought about by hard work, but not violent hard work, nor work directed at just one thing, as is the condition of athletes, but at the actions of those who are free. And these must be present in men and women alike. Pregnant women too should look after their bodies: they should not stop being active or put themselves on a slender diet. (*Pol.* 7.16.1335b2–13)

One cannot conclude that Aristotle was interested only in the 'physical condition' of girls (Lockwood 2018: 112). The case is underdetermined. After all, Aristotle doesn't provide any guidance or comment on the education of children in theoretical matters, focusing mainly on musical education in *Pol.* 7. This does not mean that he thinks children should not receive any other education, only that he did not write explicitly about it.[142] Given that both parents need to be virtuous to raise virtuous children, girls will also need to be prepared for a noble life.[143]

---

[140] Aristotle indicates at one point that women know better than men that their children are their own (*EN* 9.7.1168a26–7). He is fond of referring to a certain 'honest' horse, which tended to produce offspring resembling their sire (*Pol.* 2.3.1262a23; *HA* 9.6.586a14).

[141] See also *GA* 4.3.768b19–33.

[142] While Kraut assumes that Aristotle does not advocate literacy for girls, there is too little evidence to conclude this. '[H]e says nothing here about the education of women, because he assumes without argument that women will not be taught to read and write' (1997: 172). In fact, he says nothing about reading and writing for boys either; he mentions that musical education requires playing an instrument (*Pol.* 8.6.1340b35–40). Many girls are depicted playing instruments on vase paintings, so this may not have been educational advice only for boys.

[143] McGowan Tress (1997: 74–5, 78).

While traditional *gunakonomoi* seem to police intemperate behaviour only in older men and women, Aristotle's inclusion of them in *Politics* 7 indicates some hope for an expansion of their duties to younger individuals. For boys, the *paidonomoi* are to be involved in setting up, providing, or at least keeping track of their education. It may be that Aristotle hoped the *gunakonomoi* could take over a similar role for girl children. After all, the problems that both he and Plato identify in Sparta are not about giving women power but about not educating young girls properly.[144]

5.2 Women as Mothers

The role of citizen mothers is a powerful one. When the times comes, both parents are to study the works of physicians and natural scientists concerning the best conditions for procreation (*Pol.* 7.16.1335a39–40). There must be joint agency around the plan to conceive. Evidence from medical literature at the time points to women having considerable control over the processes of conception, pregnancy, and birth.[145] After children are born, care falls into the hands of women, particularly mothers. Very young children must be handled in the right way, move their bodies, use their voices and lungs (*Pol.* 7.17.1336a24–40) and be soothed through the correct kind of songs and stories (1336a30; 1336bb1–22). A child's cognitive abilities are present and developing as well, and are affected strongly by external influences (*EN* 2.1.1103b23–5).[146] Women are also responsible for teaching children to speak, so central to rationality and political life. Aristotle makes clear that young children will need not only stories (*muthoi*) but also 'explanations' (*logoi*) (*Pol.* 7.15.1336a31), and most of these will come from mothers and nurses.

Even in those communities where public education took place for boys, children remained under the supervision of women in the home until at least the age of seven, a formative period of child development as was recognised by

---

[144] Levy (1990, 400); *Pol.* 2.9.1269b13–1270a16. Plato remarks at *Laws* 781a: 'it is entirely wrong of you to have omitted from your legal code any provision for your women, so that the practice of communal meals for them has never got under way. On the contrary, half the human race – the female sex, the half which in any case is inclined to be secretive and crafty, because of its weakness – has been left to its own devices because of the misguided indulgence of the legislator'.

[145] The author of *On Diseases of Women* remarks: 'it requires much attention and knowledge (*epistēmē*) to bring a child to term and provide for its nourishment in the uterus, and then to give birth to it' (*Mul.* 1.25, Littré, 8.68–9). See Connell (forthcoming). While Riesbeck (2015: 150) argues that a wife's opinions are to be taken into account without this counting as joint deliberation, the case of having children seems different.

[146] On the importance of early education in *Pol.* 7 see Kraut (1997: 145–6); Sherman (1989: 151–6). It is true that without intense social interaction from early on, babies cannot develop properly.

classical philosophers.[147] One might think that Aristotle is interested only in father and sons;[148] in the *Politics*, the word '*patēr*', father, and the male version of 'child', *pais*, are employed to discuss parent/child relationships as one type of rule in the household (*Pol.* 1.3.1253b7, 10). But in the ethical works, Aristotle most often uses 'parents' (*hoi goneis*) and 'children' (*paides*) in the plural, indicating both mothers and fathers and both sons and daughters.[149] The parent provides more benefits to the child than the child can to the parent, but this relationship is not possible to equalise in a straightforward manner (*EN* 8.7.1158b12–15). This leads Aristotle to discuss a broader category into which such relationships fit, and which is hugely significant for the community as a whole: the relationship of benefactor to beneficiary (*EN* 9.7.1168a20).[150] In this context, it is the love that mothers feel for their children that serves as the paradigm of politically important connections that underlie the virtuous actions of citizens (*EN* 8.8.1158b28–35; 9.7.1168a21–5).[151]

After asserting that unequal friendships are equalised by the lesser party providing more love, Aristotle appears to take an abrupt about turn to say that actually the most virtuous person is the one that loves more, just as mothers do.

> [Friendship] seems to be in the loving rather than in the being loved. A sign of this is that mothers rejoice in loving. For some mothers give away their own children to be nursed, and loving they know them. But do not seek to be loved in return, should it not be possible to have both, but it seems to be sufficient to them, if they see/know that they do well, and they love them even though those do not render honour [to her] as a mother [being ignorant]. (*EN* 8.8.1159a28–33)

A person who loves virtuously benefits the other and in doing so enhances or expresses more fully his or her own virtuous character.

> There is the same relation between the effect and the activity, the benefited being as it were an effect or production of the benefactor. Hence in animals

---

[147] Plato *Rep.* 377c, 378a–e; *EN* 2.1.1103b23–5. Part of Plato's distrust of the elite nuclear family appears to be the character of mothers; for example, the wife of the timocratic man corrupts her son (*Rep.* 549d–e). As Pellegrin (2013: 105–6) astutely observes: 'the family is the place where future citizens are produced, and even if, according to Aristotle, the city has something to say about the education of children, there is no question of its taking the family's place in performing the task'.

[148] Karbowski (2014b: 91).

[149] E.g. *EN* 8.12.1161b18–19: 'for parents love their children as part of themselves, whereas children love their parents as the source of their being'; also 1162a3f.; 1163b17; *EN* 9.2.1165a24.

[150] In some sense, a politician or the founder of a constitution is a benefactor to all people in the city (*Pol.* 1.1.1253a30–31).

[151] *EN* 9.9 on the features of friendship brings up mothers' feelings a number of times (e.g. 1166a5–9).

their strong feelings for their offspring both in begetting them and in preserving them afterwards. And so fathers love the children – and still more
mothers – more than they are loved by them. (*EE* 7.8.1241b1–5; cf. *EN*
9.8.1168b24–5, trans. Solomon in Aristotle 1984a)

Before maturity, children are the products of their parents; this is a situation of
beneficent friendship. A child is a part of her parents due to the incompleteness
of her practical reasoning and moral understanding; the parent's guidance takes
on the role that her own complete faculties will eventually fill.

The citizen wife's role in the early education of children is sometimes
dismissed on the grounds that they would give only 'nurture' while fathers
provide more demanding moral and intellectual education.[152] But there is
little reason to put in place such a distinction.[153] Even in the education of
young children, the intelligence of citizen mothers is crucial.[154] For example,
as a young child begins to understand fairness and to feel empathy, she will
still have unruly impulses and desires. It is only by continually reinforcing
and explaining the rationale behind fair and caring behaviour that the child
can eventually gain control of their own impulses and put together
a rudimentary understanding of how to live well.[155] Virtue cannot be learned
by rote but requires expert guidance and access to exemplars (Sherman 1989:
152–4).[156]

The lives of child and parent are intertwined, even after the child has matured,
since they will think in a similar manner and share in ideas and calculations
about how to act on numerous occasions. The early decisions of the child will
be, in a way, those of the parent (*EN* 3.3.1112b278). For the parent as well, what
the achievement of the child will be is, in a way, the parent's own achievement,
having originated in their nurture and education.[157] To attribute good character

---

[152] Swanson (1992: 57–9). Lockwood (2003: 7) asserts that 'Aristotle differentiates parental roles according to sexual differences and ascribes the role of nurture to the mother, that of education to the father', but his only reference is the pseudo-Aristotelian *Oeconomica*, a text that clashes with many of Aristotle's views. For example, it advocates treating wives like slaves ('she will serve him more assiduously than if she had been a slave bought and taken home'). This is an assimilation that Aristotle carefully avoids (*Pol.* 1.2.1252b1; 1253a2–6; cf. *EN* 10.9.1180a24–9).

[153] For a more extended argument along these lines, see McGowan Tress (1997: 74–5).

[154] While Sherman details how this must be the case according to Aristotle, she sees this as hugely problematic because women are 'rationally defective'. However, women's educative role only 'sits in uneasy tension' if we accept that *akuros* indicates that women lack 'control of their passions' (1989: 154), a view that has been challenged in Section 4.

[155] For the view that Aristotle favours moral education in the home, see also Lockwood (2003: 19–21).

[156] For Aristotle, every person must be 'brought up in fine habits' (*EN* 1.4.1095b4–5). Frede (2019: 265): 'all humans require a carefully orchestrated moral and intellectual education, and training from infancy on'.

[157] Connell (2019: 188–95).

purely to genetics is a mistake Aristotle did not fall into.[158] It is not the physical health of the elite women that make intelligent children but their virtue, requiring practical wisdom, which will be the most tested in their role as mothers.[159]

5.3 Women's Share in Rule outside the Home

Within marriage, the man should not act like an oligarch (*EN* 8.10.1160b32–1161a1).[160] The preferred relation between spouses, mirrored in the broader political situation, is one of 'political' rule, where citizens equal in worth take turns to command. The idea of ruling 'in turn' (*en merei*) is a phrase that can also mean 'in part'; thus, some suggest that women have a role to play in making decisions jointly with their husbands, even if from a subordinate position.[161] The ruled-over woman thus 'influences what the ruler does' (Nichols 1992: 29–30). On this reading, decision-making takes place amongst and between participants that are equal in one sense, even though one has more decisional authority.[162]

There is evidence that wives (particularly elite wives) discussed matters of importance with their husbands and would have been expected to understand both private and public values. One example from Greek prose comes from the trial of Neaera, an 'alien' who claims to be a legitimate Athenian wife. The jurors are asked to consider their verdict in terms of what they will tell their wives and daughters:

> And when each one of you goes home, what will he find to say to his own wife or his daughter or his mother, if he has acquitted this woman? – when the question is asked you, 'Where were you?' and you answer, 'We sat as jury.' 'Trying whom?' it will at once be asked, 'Neaera,' you will say, of course, will you not? 'because she, an alien woman, is living as wife with an Athenian contrary to law, and because she gave her daughter, who had lived as a harlot, in marriage to Theogenes, the king, and this daughter performed on the city's behalf the rites that none may name, and was given as wife to Dionysus.' And you will narrate all the other details of the charge, showing how well and accurately and in a manner not easily forgotten the accusation covered each point. And the women, when they have heard, will say, 'Well, what did you

---

[158] At *Pol.* 1.2.1255b1–5, Aristotle complains about those who assume that 'a good person comes from good parents', stating that this 'frequently' (*pollakis*) does not occur. See also his misgivings about hereditary monarchy at *Pol.* 3.15.1286b22–7.

[159] Connell (2019: 183–4; 187).

[160] Oligarchy is a deviant form of constitution since its aims are misdirected towards the interest of the ruler rather than the ruled (Deslauriers 2015: 56). Better constitutions aim for the common advantage (*Pol.* 3.6.1279a18–20; Riesbeck 2015: 136–7).

[161] 'Rather than sharing by exercising authority over everything in turn, one might share by exercising authority over some things rather than others' (Deslauriers 2015: 57).

[162] Deslauriers (2015); Trott (2014: 194).

do?' And you will say, 'We acquitted her.' At this point the most virtuous of the women will be angry at you for having deemed it right that this woman should share in like manner with themselves in the public ceremonials and religious rites. (Demosthenes 59: 110–11)

This speech assumes not only that the jurors would report their public decision-making to female family members but also that these women would demand justification.[163]

This leads us to wonder if certain husbands didn't consult extensively with women on the goings-on in the city.[164] This certainly must have taken place in many elite royal families in antiquity; some wives even took on political and military roles. Three that Aristotle must have known about are Aspasia, Artemisia, and Olympia.[165] Aristotle never mentions a single female politician,[166] noting that men rule, unless something occurs contrary to nature (*Pol.* 1.12.1259b2–3).[167]

Putting aside 'unnatural' cases, then, in prescribing 'political' rule in the home Aristotle might still have in mind the need for discussions between husbands and wives. This can help to explain what he means when he says that women lack deliberative capacity. The term is most common in its political meaning – deliberative bodies within civic institutions discuss and decide together.[168]

> The deliberative factor is sovereign about war and peace and the formation and dissolution of alliances, and about laws, and about sentences of death and exile and confiscation of property, and about the audits of magistrates. (*Pol.* 4.14.1298a3–6)

---

[163] Here is a seeming case of legitimate female anger in the Greek *polis* (*pace* Harris 2001: 268–9).

[164] Xenophon hints that wives participate in broader debates. At one point he has Socrates ask Critoboulos if there is anyone to whom he talks less than his wife (*Oec.* 3.12; Clark 1982: 182). In Euripides' *Suppliants*, Theseus' mother admits it is quite unusual for a woman to try and give good advice 'openly' (*Supp.* 297–300), which suggests that they may well have done so regularly in private (Wissmann 2011: 41).

[165] On Artemisia see Hdt. *Hist.* 7.99. Olympia was the mother of Alexander the Great; Aristotle grew up in the Court of Philip II, Alexander's father. Modrak's speculation that Aristotle did not think women could rule because of his empiricism seems tenuous given such cases in his immediate proximity (1994: 218). See also Karbowski (2014a: 459): 'it is quite likely that he thought his presumption about the (naturally deficient) rational faculties of women was ... supported by the empirical facts'. See also (Mayhew 2004: 105).

[166] Although Aristotle notes the merits of the constitution of Carthage (*Pol.* 2.11.1272b24–33, 1273b26) and that the greatest of benefactors are the founders of good regimes (*Pol.* 1.1.1253a31–2), he never mentions that Carthage was founded by a woman.

[167] These unnatural cases could be women with their own property (*EN* 8.10.1160b32–1161a4). See Lockwood for an analysis of heiresses (2003: 11–12) and Mayhew (2004: 107) on other 'anomalous' women.

[168] *Pol.* 4.4.1291a27; *Pol.* 6.1.1316b30.

Deliberation is about what is up to us to do or not to do (*EN* 3.2.1111b25–6, 30; 4.2.1139b5–9) and is the source and cause of desire (*EE* 2.10.1226b19–20).[169] By figuring out what to do in varying circumstances, people are able to settle on what they want and follow through towards decisions to act.[170] In this way, a woman's unauthoritative deliberative capacity is in relation not to her internal mind but to the group situation – in which she cannot make it that her own decision affects others' actions.

When Aristotle says that women's 'deliberative capacity' is 'unauthoritative', he is referring to the lack of effectiveness of any of their opinions within an external political arena. Or rather, since the *Politics* is a normative work, he means that their deliberations ought not to be authoritative. He might recognise that Aspasia influenced Pericles, persuading him to invade Samos, and thus that the origin (*archē*) of that decision was in the wife/woman, but he indicates that this is not how things ought to be. The origin ought always to be in a man.[171] On the one hand, one might think that this means that women do not have political rule at all but just minimally 'require consultation, argument, and persuasion' (Saunders 1995: 97). On the other hand, discussion in the home can represent a case of some kind of 'shared rule' insofar as women recognise the values at stake.[172]

As we have already seen, women will deliberate and use their rationality.[173] They will ideally do so based on valuing the noble, as an expression of virtue.[174] And yet some argue that, for Aristotle, the origin of their decisions *always* lies in

---

[169] See footnote 115.

[170] On deliberation and its connection to full virtue, see Riesbeck (2015: 141–2); Connell (2019: 182–3).

[171] For a clear account of the 'origin' of decisions, see Riesbeck (2015: 136–7, 146–7). Deslauriers (2015: 48): 'To say … that men exercise rule over women is to say that men make decisions that determine the actions of women, and in that sense serve as the origin of the actions of women – or at least it is to say that this is what *should* happen'.

[172] Frank notes that this speech orientates 'interests toward a "common thing" (*Pol.* 1254a28), and thus to the constitution of a shared political association (*Pol.* 1254a18), capable of taking into account the good of the whole (*Rh.* 1354b28)' (2015: 23). Although she is not discussing marital conversations here, this idea appears to apply also in that context. Karbowski claims that because they are likened to 'assistants' to a master-craftsman, women 'are not capable of a robust, systematic grasp of the end/good of the household' (2014a: 448). While assistants in crafts may not be required to know about the ends of the overall project, this doesn't mean that they are *incapable* of understanding these. And in the case of the women in the city, Aristotle no doubt thinks it better than they do.

[173] It has been noted several times that Aristotle's comment that women ought to rest their minds when pregnant indicates that he assumes that they normally use their minds (*Pol.* 7.16.1335b16–19; Swanson 1992: 64 n.61; Kraut 1997: 154).

[174] The virtuous person aims at what is noble/fine (*EE* 8.3.1248b8–1249a17; *EN* 3.7.1115b7–24; *Metaph.* 13.3.1078a31–b6). They deliberate in light of the highest good (*EN* 6.8.1141b29–1142a10). Deliberation is for objectives achieved in the noblest manner (3.3.1112b17); it involves concern for the noble/fine (6.1.1120a23–4, 6.2.1122b6–10).

the husband – he ultimately holds the rationale for their choices.[175] In Aristotelian terms, this view is difficult to understand. If husband and wife are character friends and insofar as they are such, then they are equals in the sense of being virtuous. When they discuss matters, either those that concern the family or those political questions that the husband brings home, whatever decisions are ultimately made are *shared*. If the husband discusses the upcoming vote to go to war in the Assembly and they together discuss its merits and demerits, and based partly on this discussion the man then votes not to go to war, this decision lies partly in his wife's reasoning (*EN* 3.3.1112b26–8). Some decisions that the married couple make may even originate in the wife, for example how to care for the younger of the children.

5.4 Women's Limitations: Why No Political Rule

One of Aristotle's chief concerns in the *Politics* is the working of wider political decision-making, from which wives are to be excluded. An anecdote from history is employed to help to explain how this works: Amasis and his foot-pan.

> A husband and father, we saw, rules over wife and children, both free, but the rule differs: the rule over his children is kingly, over his wife political rule. For although there may be exceptions to the order of nature, the male is by nature fitter for command than the female, just as the elder and full-grown is superior to the younger and more immature. But in the most political states the citizens rule and are ruled by turns, for the idea of a political state implies that the natures of the citizens are equal, and do not differ at all. Nevertheless, when one rules and the other is ruled we endeavour to create a difference of outward forms and names and titles of respect, which may be illustrated by the saying of Amasis about his foot pan. The relation of the male to the female is always of this kind. (*Pol.* 1.12.1259a38–b10)

Amasis is a person from an ordinary background who became a king (Herodotus *Histories* 2.172). He explains his position to his subjects as similar to a gold foot-pan that he melted down and made into a devotional statue. The foot-pan is used to wash feet while the statue is revered. The anecdote highlights a concern that appears in many parts of the *Politics* that political rulers be encouraged to temper their tendencies to exaggerate their superiority to those they rule over.[176] Such exaggeration can lead to rebellion and instability but, in any case, it is not

---

[175] Deslauriers (2015: 60): 'He chooses not only those actions he will undertake as an individual, but also those that the household as a collective will undertake'. Against this see Scott (2020: 197).

[176] Riesbeck's (2015) reading is typical, which is that ruler and ruled in the case of political rule are distinguished by superficial appearance and not any difference in nature; see also Stauffner (2008: 936).

the best way to rule.[177] Friendship, rather than force, is what holds together political communities (*EN* 8.1.1155a22–7). As for an explanation of the permanent rule of men over women, this must lie in their different bodily forms, which are 'marks' of their different offices. Aristotle states that 'authority and subordination', those 'inevitable' and 'expedient' conditions, are 'in some cases marked out from the moment of birth' (*Pol.* 1.5.1254a23–4).[178] The bodies of men and women differ so that one is marked as inferior to the other. Deslauriers (2015: 53–55) understands the Amasis passage to indicate that, though their underlying material is the same, when the foot-pan is transformed into a statue, it becomes better in value. But what does this superiority rest in?

5.4.1 The Biological Basis for Women's Disenfranchisement

Aristotle's reasons for excluding women from the public sphere do not have to do with any intellectual incapacity. The thought that their deliberative faculty is *akuros* is normative; it is better that they submit and be trained to do so.[179] The real reason for the 'natural' inferiority of women in the political arena is due to a deficit of spirit. More spirited animals dominate less spirited ones. Women are unable to resist being controlled by more spirited men.[180] 'Ruling and being free invariably derive from this capacity', Aristotle says, 'for spirit is both imperious and indomitable' (*Pol.* 7.7.1328a6–7).[181] Men are more prone to being 'irascible' (i.e. impetuous *akrasia*), and irascible people are capable of ruling over others (*EN* 4.5.1126b1–2). This must be why 'the male', according to Aristotle, 'is more fitted to be in command than the female' (*Pol.* 1.12.1259b9). On its own, this fact cannot be a good enough reason to allow for such domination. According to Aristotle, might does not make right (*Pol.* 1.6.1255a12–40; 7.2.1324b22–3), since 'superior strength may be unjustly exercised'

---

[177] Nichols (1992) and Lindsay (1994: 135).

[178] Aristotle makes this remark when describing 'natural' slaves. As it turns out, the physical differences between these and free people are not apparent at all (1254b33–6). The difference between the sexes, however, is obvious from the moment of birth and is reinforced by cultural practices around nutrition and exercise. 'At marriage, the groom is usually bigger, strong, and much longer educated in hardiness … The visibly superior forcefulness … tempts a man unjustly to exaggerate his rule' (Levy 1990: 406).

[179] Modrak (1994: 213): 'As Aristotle puts it, the virtue of the part must have regard to the virtue of the whole, and he believes that the whole is best served by maintaining male dominance'.

[180] Dodds (1996: 85). I am sympathetic to Nielsen's idea that Aristotle's reference to Amasis's foot-pan not only illustrates a similarity between ruler and ruled but also a difference, not of intelligence or virtue, but of spirit. She writes: 'Amasis is not king because someone has to do it, but because he is a spirited general, prepared to grab power and keep it' (Nielsen 2015: 585). See also Mayhew (2004: 102), who notes that women are for Aristotle 'less able to withstand being controlled', and the account in Stauffner (2008) of the role of force in keeping women in check.

[181] According to Aristotle, this is also why Greeks can dominate Asians (*Pol.* 7.7.1326b28–33).

(1324b28).[182] Indeed, Aristotle believes that bad regimes are those that teach men to dominate rather than co-operate.[183]

So we must seek justification for male domination of women from somewhere else. In the *Politics*, Aristotle states that the fitness of men to rule (as opposed to women) is due to the fact that they are 'superior', using the term *kreitton* (*Pol.* 1.5.1254b14).[184] He later claims that the fact 'that rulers ought to be superior to the subjects cannot be disputed' (1332b34–5). The only 'metaphysical' rationale Aristotle gives for such superiority comes from his biology. In *GA* 2.1 he says that male (not the male animal) is superior to female in the abstract because it is free from the physical effects of its action (*GA* 2.1.732a3–10). *DA* 3.5.430a18–19 states that the agent is more honourable than what is acted on.[185] But this is too abstract to be of any use.

Another possible reason Aristotle could bring forward to argue for men ruling rather than women takes us back to *akrasia*. Men are more prone to *akrasia* about spirit, such as anger and indignation; women are not as prone to that sort of weakness but rather to weakness about appetites. It is open for Aristotle to argue (although he never does) that it is safer to put politics into the hands of those who are sometimes irrationally guided by spirit. Spirit is more akin to reason and is often orientated towards the good, even though it is unthinking.

> Spirit would seem to hear reason a bit, but to mishear it. It is like over-hasty servants who runs out before they have heard all their instructions, and then carry them out wrongly, or dogs who bark at any noise at all, before investigating to see if it is a friend. In the same way, since spirit is naturally hot and hasty, it hears, but does not hear the instruction, and rushes off to exact a penalty. (*EN* 7.6.1149a25–31)

This leads Aristotle to say that '*thumos* follows reason in a way (*pōs*), but appetite does not', which explains why it is less shameful to succumb to *thumos* than to experience appetitive *akrasia* (1149b15).[186] By extension one might

---

[182] Aristotle, like Plato, rejects the view that 'justice is the rule of the stronger' as expounded by, for example, the sophists Callicles and Thrasymachus.

[183] 'Imperial and "macho" cities, such as Sparta . . . educate individual citizens to seek mastery over their fellow citizens, within the city, as the city itself seeks mastery over cities within the Pan-Hellenic community' (Balot 2015: 119).

[184] Some suggest that *kreitton* means stronger and more powerful (Stauffner 2008: 935), but this is only one meaning of the term. It more often means 'superior' or 'better', as in the *GA* passage.

[185] This interpretation of the *GA* 2.1 passage, which in itself is opaque, is convincingly developed by Lefebvre (2018).

[186] Pearson (2011) thinks that *thumos* is 'inherently directed at noble ends' and reasons in a partial way. This seems difficult to maintain if reasoning is only something that happens in human beings, since the dog is here directed by *thumos*. However, there might be a way in which *thumos* directs an animal or human in line with reason. It is difficult to see, though, why *epithumia* cannot also do so, given that one might eat in order to survive, which is an end reason would choose.

consider spirited people, like the spirited part of soul, to be more straightforward and open, even when they get things wrong. Appetitive people, on the other hand, are more likely to manipulate reasoning for their own ends, leading to possible deceptiveness and scheming that would be detrimental to politics. If women are not able to gain control, which their lack of aggressive spirit would often lead to, they will be unable to intimidate others or force rule during insurrection and would have to resort to lying, scheming, and plotting to gain control. Arguably, such methods are dangerous and unattractive.[187]

However, it is possible to construct an Aristotelian view that makes the rule of spirit an even more dangerous pathology for the body politic.[188] With men solely in charge, tyranny and unjust rule is close by all the time due to the propensity to seek power over others, for 'spirit perverts rulers even when they are the best men' (*Pol.* 3.16.1287a31–2). Aristotle disdains the military virtues and the application of force (*Pol.* 7.2.1324b9–24). Spartans, for example, do not cultivate leisure. By emphasising masculine military virtues over all others, 'they are not happy people' (*Pol.* 7.14.1333b22–3).[189] In the *Nicomachean Ethics*, he makes mildness (*proatēs*) a virtue (*EN* 4.5).[190] One must lack an anger that desires revenge when the virtuous thing to do is to forgive the offence (1126a2–3). Indeed, it would seem that Aristotle disagrees with a prominent strand of thought in ancient Athens, which is that anger is the basis of power, particularly democratic power. In writing that 'we sometimes praise those who are harsh tempered as manly, and fitted to command', he does not mean that being harsh-tempered is a virtue. Indeed, the more feminine 'mildness' is much more praiseworthy.[191]

The thought that 'political leaders should ideally be calm, collected individuals who do not let their emotions interfere with their deliberation' (Karbowski 2014a: 443) shows up the flaws of *male* politicians rather than of women. As Lucrezia Marinella pointed out in the seventeenth century, according to Aristotle's theory, men 'have a greater propensity for irrational anger, and the consequent desire for revenge, which results from an unrestrained desire for honour' (Deslauriers 2019: 727). Such arguments for a preference for female rulers in early modern Italy were based on Aristotelian physiology.[192]

---

[187] Aristotle accuses women of colluding with tyrants at various points, calling them *potagogides*, procurers of information or spies (*Pol.* 5.11.1313b13, 34–8).

[188] Dodds (1996: 85).   [189] Lockwood (2018).

[190] There is an affective scale from anger to mildness (*EN* 4.5.1126a31–3; *Rh.* 2.3.1380a6–7).

[191] On anger as 'necessary' for democratic participation, see especially Allen (2003). Allen shows how problematic such a view was for the harmony of households and argues that this is what lies behind the depiction of female anger as dangerous in certain Greek tragedies.

[192] See also Dodds (1996: 74).

Dismissing abstract metaphysical and emotional rationales for barring women from rule leaves us with the idea that a lack of spirit is all that exempts them from power. Is it just to rule over women because they are those who are 'to be ruled over' (*tōn despostōn; Pol.* 7.2.1324b39)? That passage concerns 'natural slaves', and we have seen again and again that Aristotle does not think that women ought to be slaves of their husbands.[193] The real reason why men rule rather than women is due to the way that spirit controls their moral lives.[194] This requires that men have a public presence to confirm their deliberative capacities, whereas for women their virtue can be achieved in silence.

5.4.2 The Silence of Women

Let's consider once again the situation described in the *Historia Animalium*.

> Thus a woman is more compassionate and more prone to tears than a man, furthermore, more jealous and complaining and more apt to scold and hit out. The female is also more dispirited (*dusthumon*) and despondent (*duselpi*) than the male, is more shameless and lying, more inclined to deceive and has a longer memory. (8.1.608b8–13)

Why would women be in this despondent state?[195] Women, according to Aristotle, are unable to resist dominance by those stronger and more aggressive than they are (i.e. men). This explains why they are ruled over perpetually: their judgements may have intrinsic authority (they may be correct) but they lack extrinsic authority; they cannot make it so that these judgements are realised because they can neither control men nor can they act without male approval.

Jealousy, scolding, complaining, and hitting out[196] fit a person who has not been allowed to have any say at all. Thus, what Aristotle describes in the *HA* is the fact that women are intellectually and emotionally frustrated, which leads to the negative traits here described.[197] Mayhew is quite correct to note that

---

[193] Even in the case of slaves, this hardly seems a good justification in Aristotelian terms. As Kraut puts it: 'A person's defective *thumos* would be an odd reason for enslaving him; that he does not resist slavery does not show that enslaving him is just' (1997: 94).

[194] Aristotle does not use his science to justify this; it is just that what he says in his zoology about female character fits with his view about women in his political works.

[195] As the Hippocratic treatise 'On young girls' (*Virg.*) notes, more women hang themselves than men 'for womanly nature is more fainthearted and sorrowful' (*athumoterē kai lupērotēre*) (Littré 8.466).

[196] If this means physical violence then it seems out of the usual for women. One might view this, however, as an extreme reaction to stress. Xenophon famously describes Xanthippe as physically violent in the *Memoribilia*.

[197] On the effects of oppression, see Bartky (1990). In the Hippocratic works, one female patient with an illness caused by *lupē* – grief or depression – is described as 'refractory', literally one who 'cannot endure the reigns' (*Ep.* 3.17, case 11; Littré, 3.134). See Thumiger (2017: 362–5) for

a woman in ancient Greece 'had a lot ... to complain about' (2004: 105).[198] By noting this in a work collecting relevant data, Aristotle does not necessarily endorse the situation. Most rule in the city is corrupted, as explained in the central books of the *Politics* (4–6). Aristotle provides information to the potential legislator so that they can stabilise the current situation ('politicians should help existing constitutions', *Pol.* 4.1.1289a1–7). The aim of the political community, according to Aristotle, is human flourishing but, practically speaking, this is not possible in a community that is at war with itself.[199] Although he does not mention the same problems within the household, given their parallel structures, it is reasonable to suppose that just as the city cannot function properly without avoiding internal insurrection, nor can a household.[200] There is a particular difficulty in cities with men who do not have political power but think that they deserve it. A similar situation could be said exist in the home, with women who believe that they ought to have more external influence than they are currently allowed.[201] The city and household must be harmonious; thus, it is a good idea to address or at least mitigate the complaints of women in the home.

Being intelligent, women have the capacity to understand many complex, politically important matters going on around them. They can see that some of the decisions that men, or more personally, their own male relatives, are making are wrong or will lead to dangers or distresses for others. For Pseudo-Aristotle, a woman ought not to express her opinions or disagree with a husband:

> In all other matters [other than housework], let it be her aim to obey her
> husband (*viro parere*); giving no heed to public affairs. (*Oec.* 3.1.)

Women who complain are badly behaved, perhaps they are even 'plotting' against men, as depicted in several Aristophanic comedies.[202]

---

a fuller discussion of this case and others to do with depression, despondency (*dusthmiē*), and bitterness (*pikros*).

[198] See also Harris (2001: 275–6).

[199] See Balot (2015); Saxonhouse (2015). *Politics* 5 warns of all the ways that revolutions and civil strife could happen; the politician must be concerned with 'the sort of things that preserve and destroy cities' (*EN* 10.9.1181b18).

[200] '[I]n the household first we have the sources and springs of friendship, of political organization, and of justice' (*EE* 7.10.1242a36–b1).

[201] In terms of political organisation, those who are disenfranchised will feel resentment. 'Thus, [Aristotle] urges those in power to acknowledge the claims of those who have been excluded from "sharing" in the regime'. 'The art of politics, then, is to ensure that the resentments – the hostility felt toward those who have the rewards, honors, and power by those who do not – are softened insofar as is possible' (Saxonhouse 2015: 199, 201).

[202] Another example occurs in Euripides' *Hippolytus* (645–50), where it is suggested that women ought to be allowed to converse only with animals in order to prevent their 'plottings'.

On the surface, it might appear that Aristotle, like many of his contemporaries, thinks that women ought not to speak their minds. How we understand his view on this matter depends on careful consideration of a quotation he uses from Sophocles' *Ajax*.

> [I]n all cases [of gendered virtues] one ought to think like the poet who said of a woman 'to a woman silence brings orderliness (*kosmon*)' – whereas this does not apply to a man. (*Pol.* 1.13.1260a28–31)

Aristotle uses quotations from Greek literature throughout his *Politics*. Jill Frank offers a compelling way to understand these. The intended audience are well brought up men who are to be legislators and/or leaders in their community; the intention is partially rhetorical.

> What if, by incorporating this passage from 'the poets' (1252b7), as, we saw, is typical of his examples of enthymemes in the *Rhetoric*, and hence by way of 'things shared in common (*dia tōn koinōn*)' with his audience (*Rh.* 1355a28), Aristotle is opening an opportunity for his audience 'to supply for themselves' (*Rh.* 1357a18) the 'premises and subject matter (*logoi*)' (*EN* 1095a3–4) of his logos? (Frank 2015: 25)

Rhetorical enthymemes require the listener to supply their own premise to complete the argument; similarly, these quotations invite the reader to reason for themselves.[203]

The quotation from *Ajax* is thus an invitation to delve further into the difficult matter of the status of free women, so much debated at the time, particularly in tragedy.[204] Future politicians must be encouraged to bring their own ideas and thinking to such inexact matters.[205] In the case of the phrase from Sophocles' *Ajax* in which a female character, Tecmessa, is speaking to profess the recommendation that she be silent, this cannot be taken at face value. The content of the well-known play shows Tecmessa to not only be a good person, but also to be intelligent and reasonable.[206] Aristotle chose the quotation carefully; he has great respect for Sophocles, whose works reach the perfection of the tragic art

---

[203] Making such inferences constitutes part of the pleasure of poetry (*Poet.* 4.1448b9–20). On the rhetorical nature of tragedy see especially Frank (2015); Kirby (2012).

[204] Hall (1997: 103–10).

[205] The degree of exactness in ethics is suited to the subject matter (*EN* 1.3.1094b11–27; 9.2.1165a13–14). On lack of precision in political matters see Saxonhouse (2015: 201–3).

[206] The thought that ancient Greek culture generally regarded women to be irrational and impulsive while men are level-headed (e.g. Riesbeck 2015: 145) is undermined by characterisations of women in numerous tragedies. Karbowski's idea that for Aristotle there is a 'fundamental deficiency in a woman's ability to grasp the central ethical value concepts that inform the aim of human action at any level, public or private, e.g. happiness, nobility' (2014a: 449) is far-fetched given that he evokes the character of Tecmessa, who understands these ideals much better than her male partner does.

form (*Poet.* 4.1449a14–18). Furthermore, Sophocles' works are to be preferred to those of Euripides because he depicts characters as they should be, as good (*spoudaioi*), rather than as they really are.[207] We must ask, what does Aristotle want his politically engaged readers to take from this quotation? They will all have access to knowledge of this play and its allusions, so it is best to consider these first.

The story involves complex and troubled gender relations, drawing on Homer, but directed towards current Athenian laws, which distinguish legitimate from illegitimate wives and children.[208] It begins when Ajax loses the competition for his cousin Achilles' armour to the crafty Odysseus. Odysseus has outwitted Ajax through *logos*, argument. As a character, Ajax is exaggeratedly manly; he is large, like a bulwark, and a killer.[209] This manliness is undermined by his mental illness: attempting to revenge himself, he wrongly kills livestock believing them to be the enemies that robbed him of his prize. Realising his error, he kills himself. Before each bad decision, Tecmessa attempts to dissuade him. Her status as wife is ambiguous; she is of royal standing but she is 'spear bed-mate', a prize of war. But she is redeemed by his affection for her and her production of a healthy son. Within the Homeric context, she could become his wife.[210] It is when she attempts to dissuade Ajax from the first act of folly, based on sound reasoning about the good life (and in particular the honour of the family), that Ajax voices the remark she refers to: 'The orderliness of a woman is silence'.

Tecmessa tells her interlocutors that this is 'as he often said'.[211] Through this saying Ajax endeavours to *convince* Tecmessa not to try to dissuade him. This is a general statement of what she ought to do, in line with other 'orderly' women, which is to be quiet. What the statement absolutely cannot imply is that women should not speak. Refusal to speak was considered a grave illness.[212] Besides, speech for Aristotle is part of human rationality, tied to being political (*Pol.* 1.1.1253a8 f.). Women have speech to the full extent or else they could not be human.[213]

---

[207] *Poet.* 25.1460b33–5, 15.1454b6–13. Conscious of the seeming inappropriateness of Ajax as male authority and Tecmessa as immoral schemer, Nielsen speculates that Aristotle was merely interested in the 'stock phrase' and 'inadvertently stumbled over a case where received wisdom was put under pressure' (Nielsen 2015: 583). Given how carefully he selects his quotations from poetry and their purpose in a work such as this, this seems unlikely.

[208] Ormand (1996).   [209] Dutta and Easterling (2001: 1).

[210] For an excellent discussion of Tecmessa's intelligent manipulation of her position, see especially Ormand (1996).

[211] I take this to mean that it is what Ajax, a mentally ill man who ruins his life and reputation, often said to Tecmessa. I reject the view that this was a commonplace; (Simpson 1997: 68 n.13; Riesbeck 2015: 151 n.57).

[212] Thumiger (2017: 101–141).   [213] Swanson (1992: 59).

Ajax is simply wrong and may have also been wrong in the other instances when he refuses to consider the views of his sensible 'bed-mate', and especially when he goes so far as to forbid her from speaking. Her remark that 'Hearing this I gave in, and he rushed off' (*Aj.* 294) does not indicate that she has been persuaded but rather that she has been forced into submission. Clearly, Tecmessa has attempted again and again to talk to Ajax about what is important (for himself and his family) and she is repeatedly told not to talk; this shows without any doubt that Ajax is not good at communicating.[214] He neither considers Tecmessa's opinion nor even convinces her that he has done so; Ajax is bad at conversation in general and is notoriously silent in the play. For example, at 311 he is said to be 'speechless', so the chorus has to ask Tecmessa to tell them what he has done.[215]

If Aristotle means to indicate that women ought to be silent when they have good, life-saving, reputation-saving advice, this seems extraordinary indeed. The context of the play and the way Aristotle uses quotes from tragedy puts this statement into a different light. One 'hidden' message may well be that husbands ought not to be too overbearing.[216] To tell your female partner to shut up because she is giving you good advice you don't want to take is boorish and uncivilised; but worse than this, it will provoke legitimate rebellion within your own home.

Another insight comes from what Aristotle says directly after the Ajax quotation: 'the orderliness of a woman is silence', which is: 'this is not equally so for a man' (*Pol.* 1.12.1260a31). This suggests that male goodness is more strongly tied to public discourse and external approval. While women such as Antigone are able in their own minds to come to conclusions about justice, men are more likely to depend on external ratification of their views.[217] For women, in contrast, when their deliberations are nullified, as in the case of Tecmessa and that of Antigone, this does them no *moral* harm. This suggests that men will spend more time ensuring that everyone share their views and will have less time for self-reflection. This situation also fits the more spirited nature of men. Having a great deal of spirit, young men cannot be expected to develop their

---

[214] Communication requires listening as well as speaking; Ajax fails to listen. See Trott (2014: 198): 'Over and over again, Greek drama depicts the activity of women as reasoned advice and counsel in the face of violent outrage or proud obstinacy. The problem in each of these cases is that the men will not listen, so the lack of authority, or akuron, of women follows from the men's failure to listen or follow reason when it comes from a woman'. See also Saxonhouse (1985).

[215] This also contributes to his failure to win the arms of Achilles in the first place against the quick witted and smart talking Odysseus.

[216] Levy suggests the rhetorical context. 'He resorts to oblique satire, to teach that men cannot well preserve their own households and polities unless they share rule with women' (1990: 401).

[217] Sophocles' *Antigone* is depicted as claiming that burying her brother is 'just by nature', despite particular prohibition (*Rh.* 1.13.1373b9–13).

virtuous characters if they experience too much insurrection or opposition. While girls can turn the other cheek, due to a milder temperament, boys must fight to assert themselves when opposed by others.[218] This situation can be seen as a strength for women in certain circumstances; for example, if they are held captive by foreigners, they can preserve their own ideas even while under the external control of others.[219] This contrast also helps to explain why silence is so much more pathological for men than for women. Ajax's mental illness is tied up with his inability to speak and communicate, which also makes him unmanly (*Aj.* 311, 317–20). In contrast, although Tecmessa remains silent throughout the second half of the play, there is no indication that this is either because she is unduly ill or that this state will do her any harm.[220] Thus, there is more effort and responsibility required of men, making it more difficult for them to be and remain good.

5.4.3 The Nobility of Love

The character of Tecmessa in Sophocles' *Ajax* consciously mimics the role of another Homeric wife, Andromache.[221] This parallel reinforces the clash between sensitivity and spirit in the relations between men and women, which Aristotle must be alluding to. Hector is setting out to his death; Andromache, the archetypical good wife, pleads with him to consider her and their son, Astyanax (400). This speech, although appreciated by her husband, falls on deaf ears; his values are elsewhere. Hector replies:

> 'All these things are in my mind also, lady; yet I would feel deep shame before the Trojans . . . if like a coward I were to shrink aside from the fighting; and the spirit will not let me, since I have learned to be valiant and to fight always among the foremost ranks of the Trojans, winning for my own self great glory'. (*Iliad* 6.440–46, trans. Lattimore)

Despite Hector's evident affection for his young son (6.470–77), the flourishing and cohesion of his own family are not his concern; instead he seeks immortal glory as an individual, following most his aggressive 'spirit'. For Aristotle, this timocratic urge is typical of men, but without the counterbalance of those (men and women) who strive to continue the stable life of the home, no good people can populate the future. It is not only that Hector does not care for the fate of his wife as slave after his death, or only insofar as someone might mention that she is the widow of valiant Hector (6.455–65), it is that he does not seem to care for

---

[218] As Nichols puts it: 'if the deliberative element has insufficient authority in the woman, it has too much in the man' (1992: 29, 33). See also Lindsay (1994: 137).

[219] Another common theme in Greek tragedy.   [220] Ormand (1996: 57–62).

[221] Ormand (1996: 49–50).

the preservation of his own culture. The ideal wife figure for Aristotle will care for this and recognise its profound value.

For Aristotle, because of their spirited nature, 'men are more likely than women to covet honour'.[222] In his reflections on the best of people, the great-souled men (*megalopsuchos*) whose virtue falls within the purview of honour (*EN* 4.3.1124a5–6), Aristotle says that while deserved honour can be enjoyed and acknowledged, it is not in itself of much worth. 'For he does not care much even about honour, which is the greatest of external goods'. For him 'honour is a small thing' (*EN* 4.3.1124a16–19).[223] The most exemplary of 'great deeds' seem to come in two varieties – going beyond the usual when it comes to courage and being beneficent (1124b8–12).[224] It is beneficent love that takes precedence in terms of the 'good': 'being loved is enjoyed in itself; hence it seems to be more valuable (*kreittōn*) than being honoured' (*EN* 8.8.1159a25–6).[225]

From an Aristotelian perspective, the noblest person in *Ajax* would seem to be Tecmessa rather than the eponymous character. That Ajax doesn't properly understand the good of generous benefaction is clear in his hopes for his son, which belie a selfish perspective.[226] Rather than wish for him to be 'better than his father', as Hector did for Astyanax in the *Illiad* (479–80), he wishes that his son, Eurysaces, be the same as himself, only luckier (548–50). Ajax is the quintessential human draught without a draught board (*Pol.* 1.2.1253a6–7), barely counting as human in his antisocial, disconnected, pathological self-obsession (457–9). Furthermore, rather than triumphing over the more 'feminine' behaviour of Odysseus, Ajax is defeated by his lack of speech. He does not try through speech to re-establish his place in the social circle, to reinforce his self-esteem, but instead obliterates himself in suicide, securing a bad reputation for eternity.

And as the examples of Ajax and Hector illustrate, a love of honour can disrupt the drive for the highest kind of beneficent love. A good woman could then, in principle, be the sort of person who would face danger in a great cause, being willing to sacrifice her life in things that matter (1124b7), such as giving birth to new citizens. She may also be 'the sort of person who does good but is

---

[222] Swanson (1992: 61).

[223] Curzer (2012: 124–5). For more on the connection between traditional femininity and Aristotle's *megalopsuchos*, see Swanson (1992: 61–2).

[224] Curzer (2012: 128).

[225] It is interesting in the context that, although Aristotle speculates about whether Ajax is a *megalopsuchos* in the *Posterior Analytics* (97b15–25), he comes to reject this idea in the ethics, since Ajax is consumed by a concern with honour (Curzer 2012: 138).

[226] The Homeric hero desires honour and reputation above all else (Dutta and Easterling 2001), a perspective from a warrior culture critiqued by both the tragedians and Aristotle.

ashamed when [s]he receives it' and one that 'returns more good than [s]he receives' (1124b9–10), common characteristics of mothers, as Aristotle describes them.[227]

The spirited nature of men means that they have ultimate control in the household and in the city. Women are most often unable to override their decisions. Thus, a woman in such a world has to keep her own counsel and bide her time. Internally, she may indeed triumph, although her external circumstances are less secure. While Aristotle gives a show of endorsing this situation, whereby spirited men command the scene, his ethical standpoint and his ambiguity about the status of women throughout the *Politics* provides some nuance to his position. Given that spirit is hasty, violent and destabilising, it may not be so positive either in household or city. Without the sort of training in values that ensures self-controlled courage, rather than the free rein of spirit, and training all to focus on the prize of the peaceful philosophical life, rather than the honours and thrills of battle, the best life will never be within reach for anyone. But women, who lack 'wild' and dominating spirit, are closer to such a perspective already. They do not need external confirmation but can think the right thoughts and preserve the values of their culture and quietly pass these on to their children, and are thus already much closer to the ideal philosophical life.

6 The Philosophical Woman[228]

Aristotle thought women intellectually capable.[229] Although he deems women's deliberative capacity 'unauthoritative', he never mentions any deficiency in women with respect to higher cognitive capacities such as *technē*, *dianoia*, *theōria*, or *nous*.[230] In Section 2 it was established that, in terms of the physical body, female humans are well placed to achieve theoretical wisdom.[231]

---

[227] In relation to the ideal of a mother's love, Brill (2020: 236) notes: 'To find any comparable activity we would have to reach into the further horizon of noble deeds for Aristotle'.

[228] One of the main people to take seriously the implication that, for Aristotle, there is no bar on women being philosophers, is Swanson (1992: 61–5). Her treatment greatly informs this section.

[229] See, for example, *HA* 9.10.587a9–24 on the intelligence and skill of midwives. Some other examples come from the *Poetics*, where female characters experience double recognition (Iphigeneia, *Poet.* 11.1452b5–7), and others, such as Electra, use reasoning (*sullogismos*) to get there (*Poet.* 16.1455a4–5).

[230] Some who argue that women suffer moral failing admit that they do not have intellectual failing for Aristotle. See Fortenbaugh (1977); Modrak (1994: 209–10). Riesbeck (2015: 145 n.44) writes that women '*can* possess intellectual virtues'. Dodds (1996: 81) thinks that the 'call to thoughtfulness – and so to the virtues of practical and theoretical wisdom – extend every bit as much to women as to men'.

[231] Although as Mayhew (2004: 95) notes, in the passage from the *HA* which attributes superior cognitive capacities to female animals, Aristotle says nothing directly about whether women would 'be better equipped to study science or philosophy'.

The relative thinness of their skin, softness of their flesh, and clearness of their blood, combined with a lack of 'dwarfishness', makes their ability to discern differences second to none.[232] Furthermore, traits like having a 'longer memory' are crucial for theoretical pursuits (*Metaph.* 1.1.980b22–3). To assume that women would not be interested in philosophical questions pulls against the idea at the very beginning of the *Metaphysics* that *human beings* (*anthrōpoi*) desire to understand, and are first given this through their visual capacities; since women's senses will be more acute, there seems no good reason to deny them human curiosity.[233]

Of course, capacity and curiosity are not all that it takes to come to know the essences of things and pursue truth for its own sake. However, a lack of formal education does not appear to be problematic. It is unlikely that philosophy requires this, according to Aristotle. As Richard Kraut puts it: '[philosophy] will occur naturally, without special civic encouragement or training, since the curiosity present in all human beings leads a small number of them to philosophical activity, when favourable circumstances allow this to happen (*Met.* I.1 980a1, I.2 982b11–28)' (1997: 139). Another worry might be that without civic virtues, contemplation is impossible.[234] We have now seen, though, that women can have civic virtues and so there is no reason to bar them from the intellectual virtues built upon those.

One final obstacle is practicality. Perhaps women cannot gain theoretical knowledge because they die too young or age too quickly to be able to learn.[235] Aristotle held that female animals mature and then age more quickly than male ones (*HA* 9.3.583b27–9; *GA* 4.6.775a4–26). This explains their differential peak fertility (*Pol.* 7.16, 1335a26–35), but it could also allow for a woman to be more mature at eighteen than her male counterpart, which makes sense of her being ready for the responsibilities of household management and motherhood at that age. Many women lived beyond their fifties, like Socrates' mother, Phaenarete, who is clearly past the menopause.[236] Thus, a shorter life is not inevitable for women.

Perhaps, then, Aristotle thinks that women are held back from philosophy by the ancient equivalent of the pram in the hallway. But the role of women in the

---

[232] Mayhew notes that 'the connection that [Aristotle] makes between soft flesh and intelligence is not applied to females' (2004: 116), but there seems no reason why readers cannot infer this themselves.

[233] The only mention of a woman's interest in natural science in the corpus occurs in the *Historia Animalium* Book 10, of disputed authorship. On this passage see Connell (forthcoming).

[234] Rorty (1978).   [235] Segev ms.

[236] The craft of midwifery requires her to be 'no longer able to bear children' (*Th.* 149b6). Aristotle knows about the menopause (*Pol.* 7.16.1335a10; *HA* 9. 5.585b2–6), and so there must have been enough women around of such advanced years to make this inference.

elite home is not unconducive to the leisure required to pursue philosophy. Although they are busy with maintaining the correct distribution of nutrition and the production of textiles, as well as the care of children, women have extensive help in the form of nurses, tutors, and slaves. As for children, if a woman ceases to have them in her mid-thirties but lives beyond her fertile period, which ends at fifty, there would be many years after this with no children to care for in the home. There is even a servant in charge of the other servants, like a butler (*Pol.* 1.2.1255b35–7). It cannot be, then, that wives in such households were burdened by too much domestic work but, like elite women throughout the ages, they would have had time to acculturate.[237] Whereas Jane Austen's heroines took up music, needlework, or bible study, it is not impossible that the elite women Aristotle had in mind could have undertaken philosophy.

It has already been noted that Aristotle allows that some husbands and wives have virtue friendships. In his account of the best sort of friendship, which nobody can be happy without (*EN* 9.8.1170b19), he says that these friendships are rare and involve only a very few people 'living together' (8.3.1156b25; 8.5.1157b18–22; 9.9.1171a2–3; 9.9.1171a19–20). Xenophon's treatise on the home (*Oeconomicus*) includes a long section on the training of a young wife, ending with the recommendation that the married couple wake early in the morning together; for Lockwood, this time might have been spent doing philosophy (*Oec.* 1345a6–17; Lockwood 2003: 9). There is no hint of such an idea in Aristotle, however. Instead, the virtue friendship of spouses is more centred in upholding common values through raising a family. It is also unlikely that Aristotle thinks of husbands and wives when he mentions 'living together'. The ancient Greek home may even have been divided into men's and women's quarters (*Lysias* 1.9). Aristotle recommends that men do not even eat their meals at home but attend common meals (*Pol.* 7.9.1330a5–6).[238] When he talks of 'living together', he focuses on shared leisure activities.

> Some friends drink together, others play dice, while others do gymnastics and go hunting, or do philosophy. They spend their days together on whichever pursuit in life they like most; for since they want to live with their friends, they share the actions in which they find their common life. (*EN* 10.1.1172a2–8)

---

[237] Swanson (1992: 64 n.60). The importance of 'leisure' as time for intellectual pursuits, which are of intrinsic value, is also apparent in *Pol.* 7.1–3, for example 7.3.1325b14–22.

[238] The symposium, as depicted in the works of Plato and Xenophon as the scene of intense philosophical discussion, is a male dinner party; wives are not invited. Despite his seemingly more positive attitude towards philosophical women, Plato has Socrates dismiss his wife, Xanthippe, in order to concentrate on talking with his male friends on the day of his death (*Phaedo* 60a).

The activities listed at the outset, drinking, dice, gymnastics, and hunting, are not those that women in classical Greece engaged in; the addition of philosophy at the end seems to confirm that for Aristotle that too is a male-only pursuit.

Aristotle never mentions any female philosophers, despite the fame of Pericles' partner Aspasia and the presence of female students in Plato's Academy (*D.L.* 3.46–7). However, the idea that not only psychologically, but also temperamentally, Aristotle's ideal wife would fit better to the philosopher is something that one cannot help but notice.[239]

Swanson argues that the typical pursuits of men in the *polis* actually distract them from philosophical and theoretical lives. Citing *EN* 1177a27–34 and *Pol.* 1325a16–17, she notes that 'the possession of power, honor, or reputation would seem to distract a human being from contemplation'. The male life of honour-seeking and self-assertion in the public sphere 'resist[s] the quiet life essential for thought'. Full participatory citizenship actually 'reduces' men's 'opportunity and increases women's to contemplate'. 'In short, although Aristotle nowhere implies that one gender is more likely than the other to receive intuitive reason, he suggests that, if possessed, it is facilitated more by a female than by a male nature. The inclination to privacy, quietude, or a "passive" way of life is both a female and a philosophical one. The female nature does not, unlike the male nature, resist the quiet life essential for thought'. Power's demands and prerequisites undermine contemplation (*EN* 10.6.1176b18–19). In private life, where not covetous of honour, femaleness and philosophy go together.[240]

Added to those astute observations, one can also note that the mother is closer to philosopher, in her quiet and patient care for the intellectual and moral development of her children, than the warrior, who must keep reminding himself that it is the good life – and not glory, victory, or plunder – that matters most.

7 Conclusions

Aristotle's comments about women in his practical philosophy are directed towards citizen wives and the relationship between husbands and wives. The biological works focus on observations of differentiated behaviour in men and women (and male and female animals). In the latter, Aristotle picks up on the relevant *endoxon* that it is bad fate to be born a woman; tragedians show how their compassion and intelligence are systematically undermined by those in power. It is, then, a considerable challenge to make sure that 'matters

---

[239] As Lindsay (1994: 142–3) notes: 'the identification of peak virtue with political action – maleness – undervalues not only women and the *oikia*, but also, and perhaps more importantly, the theoretical life'.

[240] Swanson (1992: 62–3).

concerning women' (*ta peri tas gunaikas echonta*; *Pol.* 2.4.1270a11–12) are not mismanaged. For Aristotle, women's greater tendency to gentleness is the basis of co-operative virtues, and their sensitivity and intelligence must be directed towards the management of the household, while it is a good idea to 'listen' to their views so as to avoid sedition.

The attraction of reducing Aristotle's views on women to ancient Greek stereotypes of quiet, meek, and ignorant, or sexually voracious, ill-tempered, and conniving, does not take into account the ways in which Aristotle challenged these views and promoted harmony between the sexes.[241] And although he can sometimes be seen to follow the idea that men in his culture are to be glorified for courage, military process, and the physical ability to dominate others, the traditionally more feminine virtues of co-operation, thoughtfulness, and care, a quiet life away from political scrum, are just as, or perhaps even more, important to him.[242] There is an evident tension in his depiction of the good man, who must at once be both aggressive warrior and sensitive philosopher, which his model of the good woman avoids. Though women may be inferior when it comes to the spirit required to dominate and rule in the city, due to bodily weaknesses, they are in fact on a par with men in the features that distinguish humans from other animals, namely moral virtue, friendship, and the capacity to contemplate and thus to be truly happy.

---

[241] Surveying work in the early 1990s that challenged the view of Aristotle as straightforwardly racist and sexist, Lindsay (1994: 127) notes: 'Aristotle was anything but in bondage to Greek *weltanschauung*'.

[242] This has led some scholars to see Aristotelian ethics as more feminine than other varieties (Saxonhouse 1985; Sherman 1989; Swanson 1992).

References

Ancient Authors

Athenaeus (1937). *The Diepnosophists, Vols I-VII*. C. Gulick, tr., London: Heinemann.

Aristotle (1926). *Rhetoric*. J. Freese, ed., London: Heinemann.

(1935). *Metaphysica X-XIV, Oeconomica, Magna Moralia*. H. Tredennick, ed., Cambridge, MA: Harvard University Press.

(1936a). *On the Soul, Parva Naturalia, On Breath*. W. S. Hett, tr., Cambridge, MA: Harvard University Press.

(1936b). *Minor Works*. W. S. Hett, tr., Cambridge, MA: Harvard University Press.

(1937). *Parts of Animals, Movement of Animals, Progression of Animals*. A. Peck, tr., Cambridge, MA: Harvard University Press.

(1957). *Politica*. W. D. Ross, ed., Oxford: Clarendon.

(1965a). *De Generatione Animalium*. H. J. Drossaart Lulofs, ed., Oxford: Clarendon.

(1965b). *Historia Animalium, Books I-III*. A. Peck, tr., Cambridge, MA: Harvard University Press.

(1970). *Historia Animalium, Books IV-VI*. A. Peck, tr., Cambridge, MA: Harvard University Press.

(1984a). *The Complete Works*. J. Barnes, ed., 2 vols. Princeton, NJ: Princeton University Press.

(1984b). *Ethica Nicomachea*. I. Bywater, ed., Oxford: Clarendon.

(1991a). *Historia Animalium, Books VII-X*. D. Balme, tr., Cambridge, MA: Harvard University Press.

(1991b). *Ethica Eudemia*. J. Mingay, ed., Oxford: Clarendon.

Demosthenes (1939). *Orations, Volume VI: Orations 50–59: Private Cases. In Neaeram*. A. T. Murray, tr., Cambridge, MA: Harvard University Press.

Diogenes Laertius (1925). *Lives of Philosophers. Vol. I.* R. D. Hicks, tr., London: Heinemann.

Euripides (1912). *Vols. I–VIII*. A. Way, tr., London: Heinemann.

Herodotus (1920–25). *Histories. Vols. I-IV.* A. Godley, tr., London: Heinemann.

Homer (1951). *Iliad*, R. Lattimore, tr., Chicago, IL: University of Chicago Press.

Lysias (1957). *Speeches*. W. R. M. Lamb, tr., London: Heinemann.

Plato (1997). *Complete Works.* J. Cooper, ed., Indianapolis, IN: Hackett.

Plutarch (1914). *Lives, Vol. I.* B. Perrin, tr., London: Heinemann.

Sophocles (1994). *Ajax. Electra. Oedipus Tyrannus.* D. Kovacs, tr., Cambridge, MA: Harvard University Press.

Xenophon (1923). *Memorobilia and Oeconomicus.* E. C. Marchant, tr., London: Heinemann.

Modern Authors

Allen, D. (2003). Angry bees, wasps, and jurors: The symbolic politics of *orgê* in Athens. In S. Braund and G. Most, eds., *Ancient Anger.* Cambridge: Cambridge University Press, 76–98.

Balot, R. (2015). The 'mixed regime' in Aristotle's *Politics.* In T. Lockwood and T. Samaris, eds., *Aristotle's Politics: A Critical Guide.* Cambridge: Cambridge University Press, 103–22.

Bartky, S. (1990). *Femininity and Domination: Studies in the Phenomenology of Oppression.* New York: Routledge.

Brill, S. (2020). *Aristotle On the Concept of Shared Life.* Oxford: Oxford University Press.

Callard, A. (2021). Aristotle on deliberation. In R. Chang and K. Sylvan, eds., *The Routledge Handbook of Practical Reason.* London: Routledge, 126–43.

Clark, S. (1982). Aristotle's Woman. *History of Political Thought* 3(2), 177–91.

Cole, S. G. (2004). *Landscapes, Gender, and Ritual Space: The Ancient Greek Experience.* Berkeley: University of California Press.

Connell, S. M. (2016). *Aristotle on Female Animals: A Study of the Generation of Animals.* Cambridge: Cambridge University Press.

(2018). Review of Mariska Leunissen *From Natural Character to Moral Virtue in Aristotle. Mind* 127(507), 938–46.

(2019). Nurture and parenting in Aristotelian ethics. *Proceedings of the Aristotelian Society* 119(2), 179–200.

(2021). Thinking bodies: Aristotle on the biological aspects of human cognition. In P. Gregorić and J. L. Fink, eds., *Encounters with Aristotelian Philosophy of Mind.* London: Routledge, 223–48.

(forthcoming). Women's medical knowledge in classical antiquity. In K. O'Reilly and C. Pellò, eds., *Women Ancient Philosophers.* Cambridge: Cambridge University Press.

Curzer, H. (2012). *Aristotle and the Virtues.* Oxford: Oxford University Press.

Deslauriers, M. (2003). The virtues of women and slaves. *Oxford Studies in Ancient Philosophy* 25, 213–31.

(2009). Sexual difference in Aristotle's politics and his biology. *Classical World* 102, 215–30.

(2015). Political rule over women in Politics I. In T. Lockwood and T. Samaris, eds., *Aristotle's Politics: A Critical Guide*. Cambridge: Cambridge University Press, 47–63.

(2019). The conceptualization of masculine authority as unjust: Tyranny in 17th century Venice. *British Journal for the History of Philosophy* 27(4), 718–37.

Dillon, M. P. J. (2007). Were Spartan women who died in childbirth honoured with grave inscriptions? Whether to read *ierôs* or *lexous* at Plutarch, Lycourgos 27.3. *Hermes* 135, 149–65.

Dodds, D. (1996). Family matters: Aristotle's appreciation of women and the plural structure of society. *The American Political Science Review* 90, 74–89.

Dutta, S. and P. E. Easterling. (2001). *Sophocles' Ajax*. Cambridge: Cambridge University Press.

Dutsch, D. and D. Konstan. (2011). Women's emotions in Roman comedy. In D. Munteanu, ed., *Emotion, Genre, Gender in Antiquity*. London: Duckworth, 57–88.

Fortenbaugh, W. (1977). Aristotle on slaves and women. In J. Barnes, M. Schofield, and R. Sorabji, eds., *Articles on Aristotle 2: Ethics and Politics*. London: Duckworth, 135–39.

Frank, J. (2015). On Logos and politics in Aristotle. In T. Lockwood and T. Samaris, eds., *Aristotle's Politics: A Critical Guide*, Cambridge: Cambridge University Press, 9–26.

Frede, D. (2019). The deficiency of human nature: The task of 'Philosophy of human affairs'. In N. Kreft and G. Keil, eds., *Aristotle's Anthropology*, Cambridge: Cambridge University Press, 258–74.

Gregg, E. (2001). *Queen Anne*. New Haven, CN: Yale University Press.

Hall, E. (1997). The sociology of Athenian tragedy. In P. Easterling, ed., *The Cambridge Companion to Greek Tragedy*. Cambridge: Cambridge University Press, 93–126.

Harding, P. (2008). *The Story of Athens: The Fragments of the Local Chronicles of Attika*. New York: Routledge.

Harris, W. (2001). *Restraining Rage*. Cambridge, MA: Harvard University Press.

Huxley, A. (1932). *Brave New World*. London: Chatto and Windus.

Irwin, T. (1985) *Aristotle Nicomachean Ethics*. Indianapolis, IN: Hackett Publishing Company.

Karbowski, J. (2012). Slaves, women, and Aristotle's natural teleology. *Ancient Philosophy* 32, 323–50.

(2014a). Aristotle on the deliberative abilities of women. *Apeiron* 47(4), 435–60.

(2014b). Deliberating without authority: Fortenbaugh on the psychology of women in Aristotle's Politics. *Philosophical News* 8, 88–103.

(2019). Political animals and human nature in Aristotle's *Politics*. In N. Kreft and G. Kiel, eds., *Aristotle's Anthropology*. Cambridge: Cambridge University Press, 221–37.

Kirby, J. (2012). Aristotle and Sophocles. In K. Ormand, ed., *A Companion to Sophocles*. Oxford: Blackwell.

Kraut, R. (1997). *Aristotle Politics Books VII and VIII*. Oxford: Clarendon.

Lape, S. (2004). *Reproducing Athens: Menander's Comedy, Democratic Culture and the Hellenistic City*. Princeton, NJ: Princeton University Press.

Lefebvre, D. (2018). Aristotle's *Generation of Animals* on the separation of the sexes. In D. Sfendoni-Mentzou, ed., *Aristotle – Contemporary Perspectives on his Thought*. Berlin: De Gruyter, 75–93.

Lehoux, D. (2019). Why does Aristotle think bees are divine? Proportion, triplicity and order in the natural world. *British Journal for the History of Science* 52(3), 383–403.

Leunissen, M. (2017). *From Moral Virtue to Natural Character in Aristotle*. Oxford: Oxford University Press.

Levy, H. (1990). Does Aristotle exclude women from politics? *Review of Politics* 52(3), 397–416.

Lewis, G. (2008). Maternal mortality in the developing world: Why do mothers really die? *Obstetric Medicine* 1(1), 2–6.

Lindsay, T. K. (1994). Was Aristotle racist, sexist, and anti-democratic? A review essay. *Review of Politics* 56, 127–51.

Littré, E. (1839–61). *Oeuvres complètes d'Hippocrate*. Vols. I–X. Paris: Ballière.

Lockwood, T. (2003). Justice in Aristotle's household and city. *Polis* 20, 1–21.

(2018). Servile Spartans and free citizen soldiers in Aristotle's *Politics* 7–8. *Apeiron* 51, 97–123.

Mantel, H. (2020). *The Mirror and the Light*. London: 4th Estate.

Mayhew, R. (2004). *The Female in Aristotle's Biology: Reason and Rationalisation*. Chicago, IL: Chicago University Press.

McGowan Tress, D. (1997). Aristotle's child: Development from genesis, oikos and polis. *Ancient Philosophy* 17, 63–84.

Modrak, D. (1994). Aristotle: Women, deliberation, and nature. In B.-A. Bar On, ed., *Engendering Origins: Critical Feminist Readings of Plato and Aristotle*. Albany, NY: SUNY Press, 207–22.

Moss, J. (2012). *Aristotle on the Apparent Good*. Oxford: Oxford University Press.

Mulgan, R. (1994). Aristotle on the political role of women. *History of Political Thought* 15, 179–202.

Nichols, M. (1987). Classical perspectives on Femininity. *Review of Politics* 49, 130–33.

(1992). *Citizens and Statesmen: A Study of Aristotle's Politics*. London: Rowman and Littlefield.

Nielsen, K. (2011). Deliberation as inquiry: Aristotle's alternative to the presumption of open alternatives. *Philosophical Review* 120(3), 383–421.

(2015). The constitution of the soul: Aristotle on lack of deliberative authority. *Classical Quarterly* 65(2), 572–586.

Ogden, D. (1996). *Greek Bastardy*. Oxford: Oxford University Press.

Ormand, K. (1996). Silent by convention? Sophocles' Tekmessa. *The American Journal of Philology* 117(1), 37–64.

Pangle, T. (2013). *Aristotle's Teaching in the Politics*. Chicago, IL: Chicago University Press.

Pearson, G. (2011). Non-rational desire and Aristotle's moral psychology. In J. Miller, ed., *Aristotle's Nicomachean Ethics: A Critical Guide*. Cambridge: Cambridge University Press.

Pellegrin, P. (2013). Natural slavery. In M. Deslauriers and P. Destrée, eds., *The Cambridge Companion to Aristotle's Politics*. Cambridge: Cambridge University Press, 92–116.

(2015). Is politics science? In T. Lockwood and T. Samaris, eds., *Aristotle's Politics: A Critical Guide*. Cambridge: Cambridge University Press, 27–45.

Riesbeck, D. (2015). Aristotle on the politics of marriage: 'Marital rule' in the Politics. *Classical Quarterly* 65(1), 134–52.

Rorty, A. O. (1978). The place of contemplation in Aristotle's Nicomachean Ethics. *Mind* 347, 345–58.

Samaris, T. (2015). Aristotle and the question of citizenship. In T. Lockwood and T. Samaris, eds., *Aristotle's Politics: A Critical Guide*. Cambridge: Cambridge University Press, 123–41.

Saunders, T. J. (1995). *Aristotle: Politics Books I and II*. Oxford: Clarendon.

Saxonhouse, A. (1985). *Women in the History of Political Thought: Ancient Greece to Machiavelli*. Westport, CN: Praegar.

(2015). Aristotle on the corruption of regimes. Resentment and justice. In T. Lockwood and T. Samaris, eds., *Aristotle's Politics: A Critical Guide*. Cambridge: Cambridge University Press, 184–203.

Scott, D. (2010). One virtue too many? Aristotle's 'Politics' 1.13 and the 'Meno'. In V. Harte, M. M. McCabe, R. Sharples, and A. Sheppard, eds.,

Aristotle and the Stoics Reading Plato. Bulletin of the Institute of Classical Studies, Suppl. Vol. 107: 101–22.

(2020). *Listening to Reason in Plato and Aristotle*. Oxford: Oxford University Press.

Seğev, M. (draft paper) Aristotle on the bodily proportions, longevity and intelligence of women and men.

Sherman, N. (1989). *The Fabric of Character: Aristotle's Theory of Virtue*. Oxford: Oxford University Press.

Simpson, P. L. P. (1997). *The Politics of Aristotle*. Chapel Hill, NC: Chapel Hill Press.

Smith, N. (1983). Plato and Aristotle on the nature of women. *Journal of the History of Philosophy* 21(4), 467–78.

Stauffner, D. J. (2008). Aristotle's account of the subjection of women. *Journal of Politics* 70, 929–41.

Swanson, J. (1992). *The Public and Private in Aristotle's Political Philosophy*. Ithaca, NY: Cornell University Press.

Thumiger, C. (2017). *A History of the Mind and Mental Health in Classical Greek Medical Thought*. Cambridge: Cambridge University Press.

Trott, A. (2014). *Aristotle on the Nature of Community*. Cambridge: Cambridge University Press.

Wiggins, D. (1975). Deliberation and practical reason. *Proceedings of the Aristotelian Society* 76, 29–viii.

Wissman, J. (2011). Cowardice and gender in the Iliad and Greek tragedy. In D. L. Munteanu, ed., *Emotion, Genre and Gender in Classical Antiquity*. London: Duckworth, 35–55.

Acknowledgements

I warmly thank audiences in Berlin, London, and Oxford for enlightening discussion. I am most especially grateful to Mor Segev, Chiara Blanco, Rosanna Omitowoju, Catharine Edwards, Susanna Bobzien, Amanda Greene, Elena Cagnoli-Fieccone, and Fiona Leigh. I am likewise grateful to series editor James Warren and the Press's reviewer for their excellent suggestions.

Ancient Philosophy

James Warren

University of Cambridge

James Warren is Professor of Ancient Philosophy at the University of Cambridge. He is the author of *Epicurus and Democritean Ethics* (Cambridge, 2002), *Facing Death: Epicurus and his Critics* (2004), *Presocratics* (2007) and *The Pleasures of Reason in Plato, Aristotle and the Hellenistic Hedonists* (Cambridge, 2014). He is also the editor of *The Cambridge Companion to Epicurus* (Cambridge, 2009), and joint editor of *Authors and Authorities in Ancient Philosophy* (Cambridge, 2018).

About the Series

The Elements in Ancient Philosophy series deals with a wide variety of topics and texts in ancient Greek and Roman philosophy, written by leading scholars in the field. Taking a theme, question, or type of argument, some Elements explore it across antiquity and beyond. Others look in detail at an ancient author, a specific work, or a part of a longer work, considering its structure, content, and significance, or explore more directly ancient perspectives on modern philosophical questions.

Cambridge Elements ☰

Ancient Philosophy

Printed in the United States
by Baker & Taylor Publisher Services